MUSIC ★ ICONS

DYLAN

LUKE CRAMPTON & DAFYDD REES
WITH WELLESLEY MARSH

TASCHEN

HONG KONG KÖLN LONDON LOS ANGELES MADRID PARIS TOKYO

CONTENTS

8
BOB DYLAN: FREEWHEELIN'

20
CHRONOLOGY

24
THE 1960^S

92
THE 1970^S

116
THE 1980^S

1

BOB DYLAN
FREEWHEELIN'

FREEWHEELIN'

FREEWHEELIN'

BOB DYLAN: FREEWHEELIN'

In an age when the words *genius* and *icon* are so casually tossed around, few recording artists can lay genuine claim to either description. Irrespective of any music lover's subjective feelings about his or her favorite music and musicians, it is difficult for anyone not to agree that Bob Dylan is the most profound and influential singer-song-writer in the history of rock.

Born Robert Allen Zimmerman on May 24, 1941, in Duluth, Minnesota, he played in several high-school bands while attending Hibbing High School. Leaving school in 1959 (listing his ambition "To join Little Richard" in the school's yearbook), he briefly joined pop vocalist Bobby Vee's backing band (on piano) for a few gigs under the name Elston Gunnn (with three n's) the same year.

Partly grounded in gospel, blues, country and the roots of rock 'n' roll, it was the dust bowl folk of Woody Guthrie (and later the blues song structure of Robert Johnson) that most inspired him. Strumming a double-O Martin acoustic guitar (for which he had traded his electric guitar), Zimmerman began playing solo gigs around the campus while attending the University of Minnesota from the autumn of 1959, switching his name to Bob Dylan (inspired by the poet Dylan Thomas—he legally changed his name in August 1962) while performing as part of the local Dinkytown folk and coffeehouse circuit in 1960 where he would usually earn three to five dollars per performance.

Electing to leave university at the end of his first year, Dylan moved to Greenwich Village in New York City in January 1961 and regularly visited the seriously-ill Guthrie in Greystone Hospital in Morristown, New Jersey. Quickly becoming a pioneering fixture on the nascent Greenwich Village folk scene—notably at Gerde's Folk City on West 4th Street—Dylan garnered strong reviews in the local press including **The New York Times**.

Increasingly popular among fellow musicians, Dylan was asked by Columbia Records recording artiste, Carolyn Hester, to perform harmonica on her new album, and through her met Columbia Records executive/producer John Hammond at an informal audition at Hester's apartment on September 14, 1961. This led to Dylan being signed by Hammond to Columbia in October 1961, and his first album release—mostly blues and folk covers recorded over three days in November—**Bob Dylan** the following year. Keen to develop and record his own compositions, his sophomore effort, **The Freewheelin' Bob Dylan** proved to be a stunning critical and commercial breakthrough containing 11 self-penned future classics and two covers. Several of them *(Blowin' In The Wind, I Shall Be Free, Talking World War III Blues)* were coined "protest songs" by critics—a label which would (uncomfortably) stick with the artist as he became an involuntary leading light of the counterculture decade and civil rights movement which hallmarked the 1960s—a role he began eschewing as early as 1963.

Uncomfortable with rules, labels and a reluctant spokesman for anything, Dylan would subsequently challenge both himself and his audience with frequent stylistic, religious, philosophical and musical evolutions, evidenced most obviously by his much-publicized switch from acoustic to electric performance in 1965 and by his (temporary) born-again conversion to Christianity in 1979. In many ways, however, the early career trilogy of **The Freewheelin' Bob Dylan** and its two equally seminal followup albums, **The Times They Are A-Changin'** and **Another Side Of Bob Dylan** effortlessly displayed the qualities which would distinguish much of his career as a songwriter of iconic quality: unparalleled skill as a wordsmith of endless fertility and imagination; cunning often cynical humor; rich, visionary themes; anti-establishment verve; and beautiful, passionate melancholic insights on the subject of love *(Girl From The North Country* and *To Ramona)*. Added to this, a deft ability as a superb harmonicist and a unique vocal style unheard before or since his arrival.

While the highlights of his remarkable career follow in the form of images and biographical notes in this book, it is hard to recall a singer-songwriter who has had more impact and influence on that genre. Perfectly melding two traditional American music genres of folk and blues, he re-energized both and created his own unique legacy. Though a legendary performer and recording artist, it is Dylan's songwriting chops that have elevated his legend among his peers. His influence over the great majority of male and female songwriters who followed cannot be overstated.

After more than four decades and 40-plus studio and live album releases, he continues to add to an unrivaled canon of work which frequently sidesteps labels or repetition. He relentlessly tours—despite a serious illness in 1997 during which he wrote one of his least-recognized classics, the morbid and epic *Not Dark Yet.* With a steady stream of awards and honors hallmarking his entire career, Dylan was honored in April 2008 as the first rock 'n' roll recipient of the Pulitzer Prize.

Wry, impenetrable and defying categorization, how fitting it is that it took five actors and one actress to portray Dylan in the 2007 motion picture, "I'm Not There". In providing an ever provocative soundtrack to modern culture for nearly half a century, he has become a cornerstone of popular music. One life, so many colors: singer, songwriter, musician, poet, author, dee-jay, painter: Elusive, American, Icon. Ring Them Bells indeed.

BOB DYLAN: FREEWHEELIN'

Heutzutage werden die Bezeichnungen „Genie", „Ikone", „Ausnahmekünstler" inflationär verwendet, dabei gibt es nur wenige Musiker, die diese Charakterisierung wirklich für sich beanspruchen können. Wenn man persönliche Vorlieben einmal ausklammert, kann kein Musikliebhaber abstreiten, dass Bob Dylan der tiefsinnigste und einflussreichste Singer-Songwriter in der Geschichte der Rockmusik ist.

Bob Dylan wurde als Robert Allen Zimmerman am 24. Mai 1941 in Duluth, Minnesota, geboren. Er spielte in mehreren Schulbands, während er die Hibbing High School besuchte, an der er 1959 seinen Abschluss machte (im Jahrbuch der Schule gab er als Berufswunsch an: „bei Little Richard mitspielen"). Im selben Jahr hatte er unter dem Namen Elston Gunnn (mit drei n) einige Auftritte als Background-Pianist mit dem Popsänger Bobby Vee.

Gospel, Blues, Country und die Ursprünge des Rock 'n' Roll prägten Bob Dylan, doch den stärksten Einfluss übte der „Dust-Bowl-Folk" von Woody Guthrie auf ihn aus, später auch die Blues-Songs von Robert Johnson. Bei seinen ersten Soloauftritten auf dem Campus der University of Minnesota, an der er ab Herbst 1959 studierte, schrammelte Robert Zimmerman auf einer akustischen Martin Double-O, die er gegen seine E-Gitarre eingetauscht hatte. 1960 nahm er den Namen Bob Dylan an – inspiriert von dem britischen Dichter Dylan Thomas – und ließ im August 1962 seinen Namen offiziell ändern. Er spielte in den Folkkneipen im Stadtteil Dinkytown, wo er für gewöhnlich drei bis fünf Dollar pro Auftritt verdiente.

Nach dem ersten Jahr an der Uni gab Bob Dylan das Studium auf und zog im Januar 1961 in den New Yorker Stadtteil Greenwich Village, von wo aus er den im Sterben liegenden Woody Guthrie regelmäßig im Greystone Hospital in Morristown, New Jersey, besuchte. Bob Dylan wurde schnell zum Pionier der gerade im Entstehen begriffenen Folkszene in Greenwich Village – besonders häufig trat er im Gerde's Folk City an der West 4th Street auf. Er erntete positive Kritiken, unter anderem auch in der **New York Times**.

Bald war Bob Dylan bei anderen Musikern sehr beliebt; die Sängerin Carolyn Hester fragte ihn, ob er auf ihrem neuem Columbia-Records-Album nicht Mundharmonika spielen wolle. Bei einer Session in ihrem Apartment lernte er am 14. September 1961 den Columbia-Produzenten John Hammond kennen, der ihn im Oktober 1961 unter Vertrag nahm. Sein erstes Album mit dem Titel *Bob Dylan* – größtenteils Coverversionen von Blues- und Folknummern, die innerhalb von drei Tagen im November aufgenommen worden waren – erschien im Jahr darauf. Bob Dylan wollte seine eigenen Kompositionen schreiben und aufnehmen, seine zweite Platte *The Freewheelin' Bob Dylan* mit zwei Coverversionen und elf selbst geschriebenen Songs, die allesamt zu Klassikern wurden, erwies sich als Riesenerfolg bei Kritik und

Publikum. Mehrere Songs *(Blowin' In The Wind, I Shall Be Free, Talking World War III Blues)* wurden von den Rezensenten als „Protestsongs" bezeichnet. Dieses Image haftete Bob Dylan lange Zeit an, ob er wollte oder nicht, er wurde zu einer Leitfigur der Subkultur und der amerikanischen Bürgerrechtsbewegung in den 1960ern – eine Rolle, der er sich aber schon ab 1963 zu entziehen versuchte.

Dogmen und Kategorien behagten Bob Dylan nicht, er wollte sich durch nichts und niemand als Fürsprecher vereinnahmen lassen und forderte sich selbst und sein Publikum von nun an immer wieder durch Veränderungen seines Stils und seiner religiösen, philosophischen und musikalischen Überzeugungen heraus. Besonders markante Wendepunkte waren der in der Öffentlichkeit viel diskutierte Wechsel von der akustischen zur elektrischen Gitarre 1965 und seine (vorübergehende) Hinwendung zum Christentum 1979. In vielerlei Hinsicht zeigten sich in seiner frühen Trilogie aus **The Freewheelin' Bob Dylan** und den beiden gleichermaßen zukunftweisenden Folgealben **The Times They Are A-Changin'** und **Another Side Of Bob Dylan** bereits alle Qualitäten, die seine Karriere als Songwriter-Ikone auszeichnen sollten: seine unerreichten Fähigkeiten als Wortschmied mit einer unerschöpflichen Fantasie, einem durchtriebenen, oft an Zynismus grenzenden Humor, visionären Themen, einem ausgeprägten Willen zur Bekämpfung des Establishments und schönen, leidenschaftlich melancholischen Einsichten in die Liebe *(Girl From The North Country* und *To Ramona).* Hinzu kommt seine Gewandtheit als großartiger Mundharmonikaspieler und ein einmaliger Vokalstil, den man vor ihm so noch nie gehört hatte.

Die Höhepunkte von Bob Dylans bemerkenswerter Karriere sind in Form von Bildern und biografischen Anmerkungen in diesem Buch festgehalten. Niemand hätte einen größeren Einfluss als Singer-Songwriter ausüben können. Er verschmolz zwei traditionelle Genres amerikanischer Musik – Folk und Blues – miteinander, gab beiden neue Energie und schuf ein einzigartiges Vermächtnis. Seine Liveauftritte und seine Studioeinspielungen sind legendär, doch zur eigentlichen Legende wurde er durch seine Fähigkeiten als Songwriter. Generationen nach ihm folgender Songwriter hat er entscheidend geprägt.

Nach vier Jahrzehnten im Geschäft und über 40 Studio- und Livealben baut er sein beispielloses Lebenswerk weiter aus, ohne sich zu wiederholen, und lässt sich bis heute in keine Schublade zwängen. Unermüdlich geht er weiter auf Tournee – trotz einer schweren Erkrankung im Jahr 1997, während der er jenen bis heute unterschätzten Klassiker schrieb: den morbiden, epischen Song *Not Dark Yet.* Die Flut von Preisen und Auszeichnungen riss während seiner gesamten Karriere nicht ab; als erstem Rock 'n' Roll-Musiker wurde Bob Dylan im April 2008 der Pulitzer-Preis verliehen.

So ironisch und undurchschaubar dieser Künstler ist, der sich jeglicher Kategorisierung entzieht, war es nur passend, dass im Kinofilm „I'm Not There" (2007) fünf Schauspieler und eine Schauspielerin zur Darstellung von Bob Dylan herangezogen wurden. Seit fast einem halben Jahrhundert sorgt er für den stets provokanten Soundtrack zur Gegenwartskultur; er ist einer der Ecksteine der Populärmusik. Ein Leben, so viele Facetten: Sänger, Songwriter, Musiker, Dichter, Schriftsteller, Diskjockey, Maler, Amerikaner, Ikone. Und immer schwer zu fassen. „Läutet die Glocken", ja – „Ring Them Bells".

BOB DYLAN: FREEWHEELIN'

À une époque où les mots «génie» et «icône» sont souvent galvaudés, peu d'auteurs-compositeurs-interprètes peuvent légitimement prétendre à de tels qualificatifs. Quels que soient les sentiments subjectifs des mélomanes à l'égard de leurs styles de prédilection ou de leurs musiciens préférés, rares sont ceux qui ne considèrent pas Bob Dylan comme le chanteur le plus profond et le plus influent de l'histoire du rock.

Né Robert Allen Zimmerman le 24 mai 1941 à Duluth (Minnesota), il joue dans plusieurs groupes amateurs du lycée Hibbing, qu'il quitte en 1959 («pour aller rejoindre Little Richard», comme il l'indiquera lui-même dans l'annuaire de l'école). La même année, il intègre le groupe du chanteur pop Bobby Vee (au piano) pour quelques concerts, sous le nom d'Elston Gunnn (avec trois «n»).

Dylan puise ses influences dans le gospel, le blues, la country et les racines du rock'n'roll, mais il est surtout inspiré par le folk contestataire de Woody Guthrie (puis par la structure mélodique du blues de Robert Johnson). Zimmerman échange sa guitare électrique contre une Martin double-O acoustique et commence à donner des concerts en solo sur le campus de l'université du Minnesota, où il étudie à partir de l'automne 1959. Il prend alors le nom de Bob Dylan (en hommage au poète Dylan Thomas – il changera officiellement d'état civil en août 1962) et entame en 1960 une tournée dans les cafés folk de Dinkytown qui lui rapporte entre trois et cinq dollars par soirée.

À l'issue de sa première année, Dylan quitte l'université et s'installe à New York, dans le quartier de Greenwich Village, en janvier 1961. Il rend alors de nombreuses visites à Guthrie, qui vit ses derniers jours à l'hôpital Greystone de Morristown (New Jersey). Il devient rapidement une figure de la toute jeune scène folk du Village – il se produit régulièrement, entre autres, au Gerde's Folk City, sur la West 4th Street – et recueille des critiques élogieuses dans la presse locale, notamment dans le **New York Times**.

Dylan est de plus en plus populaire parmi ses confrères musiciens et Carolyn Hester, une chanteuse produite par Columbia Records, lui demande de l'accompagner à l'harmonica sur son nouvel album. C'est chez elle qu'il rencontre l'un des grands patrons de Columbia, John Hammond, le 14 septembre 1961. Peu après cette audition informelle, en octobre, Hammond lui fait signer un contrat avec Columbia. En novembre, en l'espace de trois jours, il enregistre son premier album, **Bob Dylan** – composé principalement de reprises de standards du folk et du blues – qui sort l'année suivante. Dylan a hâte d'enregistrer ses propres compositions. Son deuxième opus, **The Freewheelin' Bob Dylan** – onze titres originaux, tous de futurs classiques, et deux reprises – connaît un succès critique et commercial foudroyant, tandis que plusieurs titres sont qualifiés de «chansons contestataires» (*Blowin' In The Wind*, *I Shall Be Free*, *Talking World War III Blues*). Sa maison de disque continue à soutenir Dylan, qui devient malgré lui le symbole de la contreculture des années 1960 et du mouvement pour les droits civiques – un rôle qu'il rejettera dès 1963.

Dylan n'aime ni les règles ni les étiquettes, et rejette l'idée d'être le porte-voix de quelque cause que ce soit. Il ne cesse de se remettre en question et déroute son public par les fréquentes évolutions de son style et de ses opinions sur la religion, la philosophie et la musique. Ses revirements les plus flagrants sont son passage (très commenté) à la guitare électrique en 1965 et sa conversion (temporaire) au christianisme en 1979. Mais avec la trilogie de ses débuts – **Freewheelin' Bob Dylan** et les deux albums tout aussi mythiques qui suivront, **The Times They Are A-Changin'** et **Another Side Of Bob Dylan** – Dylan démontre déjà une aisance et des aptitudes qui l'élèveront rapidement au rang d'icône : un talent incomparable d'orfèvre des mots servi par une imagination d'une fertilité infinie, un humour acéré, souvent cynique, des thèmes riches et visionnaires, une verve contestataire et une perception magnifique, passionnée et mélancolique de l'amour (*Girl From The North Country* et *To Ramona*) – ainsi, bien sûr, que son habileté à l'harmonica et son style vocal unique et inégalé jusqu'à ce jour.

Aucun autre auteur-compositeur-interprète n'a eu autant d'impact que Dylan sur le folk et le blues, comme le montre ce livre, dans lequel les grands moments de sa carrière se suivent sous forme d'images et de notes biographiques. En fusionnant ces genres américains traditionnels, il leur a insufflé une nouvelle vie. Bien qu'il soit connu pour ses performances sur scène et en studio, ce sont les qualités d'auteur de Dylan qui ont fait naître et perdurer sa légende, et nourri l'admiration d'une grande majorité des auteurs-compositeurs actuels.

Après plus de quarante ans de carrière et plus de quarante albums, il continue à enrichir un répertoire inégalé, échappant inlassablement à la redite. Il n'a jamais déserté la scène, malgré la grave maladie qui l'a frappé en 1997, l'année où sort un de ses classiques les moins connus, l'épique et morbide *Not Dark Yet*. Sa carrière est jalonnée de nombreuses récompenses, dont la mention spéciale décernée en avril 2008 par le jury du Prix Pulitzer pour l'ensemble de son œuvre.

Narquois et impénétrable, Dylan échappe à toute catégorisation ; il n'est pas étonnant qu'il ait fallu cinq acteurs et une actrice pour l'incarner dans «I'm Not There», le film sorti sur les écrans en 2007. En composant depuis près d'un demi-siècle la «bande originale» (toujours provocatrice) de la culture moderne, Bob Dylan s'est imposé comme un pilier incontournable de la musique pop et une icône aux multiples facettes : chanteur, compositeur, musicien, poète, auteur, DJ, peintre, insaisissable, américain... Qu'on se le dise ! («Ring Them Bells», comme le dit la chanson.)

2
CHRONOLOGY

CHRONOLOGIE

CHRONOLOGIE

Barbara Yeshe

Robert Zimmerman

Shirley Zubich

Stephen LeDoux

"WE'LL REMEMBER ALWAYS..."

Barbara Yeshe: not for long—F.N.A. 3, 4; F.H.A. 2, 3; F.B.L.A. 4; Schubert Chorus 2; Pep Club 2.

Robert Zimmerman: to join "Little Richard"— Latin Club 2; Social Studies Club 4.

Shirley Zubich: not least, but usually last— F.N.A. 3, 4; F.B.L.A. 3, 4; Masquers 3, 4; Social Studies Club 4; Pep Club 4; Girls' League 3; Jr.-Sr. Prom Committee 3; "Stag Line" production 3.

Stephen LeDoux: to do better with each passing day—

Margaret Spinelli: forever having her seat changed—F.B.L.A. 3; Jr. Red Cross 3; Pep Club 2, 3; Girls' League 2; Jr.-Sr. Prom Committee 3.

Best Figure and Physique
Ione Margo, Mike Minelli

Nancy Edwards

Michael Friend

Margaret Spinelli

Robert Zimmerman

THE 1960^S

DIE 1960ER

LES ANNÉES 1960

"I been travelin' around the country, followin' in Woody
Guthrie's footsteps. Goin' to the places he went to. All I got is
my guitar and that little knapsack. That's all I need."
„Ich bin Woody Guthrie durchs ganze Land
hinterhergereist, weil ich in seine Fußstapfen treten wollte.
Ich bin dahin gegangen, wo er war. Nur mit meiner Gitarre
und dem kleinen Rucksack. Mehr brauche ich nicht."
« J'ai parcouru le pays sur les traces de Woody Guthrie.
J'ai foulé les mêmes endroits que lui. Tout ce que j'ai, c'est ma
guitare et ce petit baluchon. C'est tout ce dont j'ai besoin. »
BOB DYLAN

TUESDAY, JANUARY 24, 1961

Having arrived in New York City, 19-year-old Dylan takes the subway to Cafe Wha? on the corner of Mac-Dougal Street and Minetta Lane in Greenwich Village. After asking owner Manny Roth whether he could perform, he sings a couple of songs at their hootenanny night.

Nach seiner Ankunft in New York City fährt der 19-jährige Bob Dylan mit der U-Bahn zum Cafe Wha? an der Ecke MacDougal Street und Minetta Lane in Greenwich Village. Er fragt den Besitzer Manny Roth, ob er auftreten darf, und singt bei der Hootenanny Night ein paar Songs.

Arrivé à New York à 19 ans, Dylan prend le métro jusqu'au Cafe Wha? à l'angle de MacDougal Street et de Minetta Lane, dans le quartier de Greenwich Village. Avec l'autorisation du propriétaire, Manny Roth, il chante quelques chansons lors d'un *hootenanny* (micro-ouvert pour les chanteurs de folk).

WEDNESDAY, APRIL 5, 1961

First paid gig—$20—at the Loeb Music Center for New York University's Folk Society. Among those in the audience is Suze Rotolo, who will become the subject of his songs *Don't Think Twice, It's All Right, One Too Many Mornings*, and *Tomorrow Is A Long Time*.

Erster bezahlter Gig – 20 Dollar – im Loeb Student Center für die Folk Society der New York University. Im Publikum sitzt Suze Rotolo, der er später die Songs *Don't Think Twice, It's All Right, One Too Many Mornings* und *Tomorrow Is A Long Time* widmen wird.

Premier cachet – 20 dollars – au Loeb Music Center, pour la Folk Society de l'université de New York. Dans le public se trouve Suze Rotolo, le sujet de ses chansons *Don't Think Twice, It's All Right, One Too Many Mornings* et *Tomorrow Is A Long Time*.

TUESDAY, APRIL 11, 1961

First residence—a two-week booking—at Gerde's Folk City, on 11 West 4th Street in Greenwich Village, opening for bluesman John Lee Hooker and performing traditional fare like *The House Of The Rising Sun* as well as his own songs, including *Song For Woody*—a tribute to Woody Guthrie. He earns $90 a week.

Erstes Dauerengagement – zwei Wochen lang im Gerde's Folk City an der 11 West 4th Street in Greenwich Village, im Vorprogramm von Bluessänger John Lee Hooker, mit Folk-Traditionals wie *The House Of The Rising Sun* und eigenen Stücke wie *Song For Woody*, einer Hommage an Woody Guthrie. Er verdient 90 Dollar pro Woche.

Première résidence – un contrat de deux semaines – au Gerde's Folk City, situé au n° 11 de la West 4th Street, à Greenwich Village ; il y assure la première partie du chanteur de blues John Lee Hooker et interprète des classiques comme *The House Of The Rising Sun*, ainsi que ses propres chansons, notamment *Song For Woody* – un hommage à Woody Guthrie. Ce cachet lui rapporte 90 dollars par semaine.

SATURDAY, NOVEMBER 4, 1961

At this performance to a less-than-quarter-full hall at New York's Carnegie Chapter Hall Folklore Center, mainly staged as a showcase for company executives following his signing to Columbia, Dylan performs seven songs (a mix of Bukka White, Lead Belly, Guthrie, and Bessie Smith). He reportedly earns $20.

Bei seinem Auftritt im weniger als zu einem Viertel besetzten Carnegie Chapter Hall Folklore Center in New York spielt Dylan nach seinem Signing bei Columbia, quasi als Showcase für die Chefetage, und singt sieben Lieder (eine Mischung aus Bukka White, Lead Belly, Guthrie und Bessie Smith), wofür er angeblich 20 Dollar bekommt.

Dylan joue sept titres (mêlant Bukka White, Lead Belly, Guthrie et Bessie Smith) au cours de ce concert, organisé après sa signature chez Columbia dans une salle aux trois quarts vide du Carnegie Chapter Hall Folklore Center, à New York, devant un parterre composé principalement des patrons du label. Il aurait été payé 20 dollars.

THE FOLKLORE CENTER

Presents

BOB DYLAN

IN HIS FIRST NEW YORK CONCERT

SAT. NOV. 4, 1961   8:40pm

CARNEGIE CHAPTER HALL

154 WEST 57th STREET • NEW YORK CITY

All seats $2.00

Tickets available at: The Folklore Center
110 MacDougal Street
New York City 12, New York

GR 7 - 5987

MONDAY, NOVEMBER 20, 1961

Having signed a five-year contract with Columbia Records on October 26, and with only a guitar and a harmonica as accompaniment, he cuts nine tracks, including *Man Of Constant Sorrow* and *Ramblin' Blues*, in a session lasting nearly three hours at Columbia's New York Studios. He will return Wednesday afternoon to record more tracks, both sessions composing his debut LP—the self-titled **Bob Dylan**. Producer John Hammond's off-the-cuff comment that the album cost "about $402" will go into folklore.

Nach der Unterzeichnung eines Fünf-Jahres-Vertrags bei Columbia Records am 26. Oktober nimmt er, nur begleitet von Gitarre und Mundharmonika, in einer dreistündigen Session in den New Yorker Columbia Studios neun Stücke auf, darunter *Man Of Constant Sorrow* und *Ramblin' Blues*. Am Mittwochnachmittag kommt er wieder und nimmt die restlichen Stücke auf, aus den beiden Sessions entsteht seine Debüt-LP – von ihm selbst **Bob Dylan** genannt. Die Bemerkung von Produzent John Hammond, das Album habe „ungefähr 402 Dollar" gekostet, geht in die Musikgeschichte ein.

Après avoir signé un contrat de cinq ans avec Columbia Records le 26 octobre, il enregistre neuf titres accompagnés uniquement de son harmonica et de sa guitare, notamment *Man Of Constant Sorrow* et *Ramblin' Blues*, au cours d'une séance de près de trois heures dans les studios new-yorkais de Columbia. Il y revient le mercredi après-midi pour enregistrer d'autres titres ; ces deux sessions donnent naissance à son premier album – l'éponyme **Bob Dylan**. La remarque spontanée de son producteur, John Hammond, sur le fait que l'album aurait coûté « environ 402 dollars » entrera dans la légende.

"Resembling a cross between a choir boy and a beatnik Mr. Dylan has a cherubic look and a mop of tousled hair he partly covers with a Huck Finn black corduroy cap ... both comedian and tragedian ... his music-making has the mark of originality and inspiration ... but it matters less where he has been than where he is going."

„Mit seinem engelhaften Gesicht und dem strubbeligen Haarschopf, den er zum Teil mit einer schwarzen Huckleberry-Finn-Kordmütze bedeckt, sieht Mr. Dylan aus wie eine Kreuzung aus Chorknabe und Beatnik ... komisch und tragisch zugleich ... seine Musik ist originell und zeugt von einer besonderen Inspiration ... doch interessanter noch als die Frage, wo er das hernimmt, ist die Frage, wie er sich weiterentwickeln wird."

« Avec ses allures d'enfant de chœur mâtiné de beatnik, M. Dylan ressemble à un chérubin, coiffé d'une casquette en velours côtelé à la Huckelberry Finn qui vient écraser sa touffe de cheveux ébouriffés... à la fois comédien et tragédien... sa musique est marquée par l'originalité et l'inspiration... Mais là d'où il vient compte moins que là où il va. »

ROBERT SHELTON, THE NEW YORK TIMES, SEPTEMBER 29, 1961

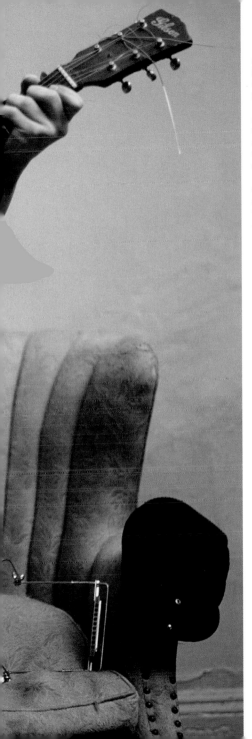

"This reviewer has to say that the record seems to be one of the best to come from the boiling folk pot in a long, long time. One reason is that Dylan is blessed with a gift of style— individual dynamic style!"

„Der Kritiker muss gestehen, dass diese Schallplatte das Beste zu sein scheint, was seit sehr, sehr langer Zeit aus dem brodelnden Folkloretopf gekommen ist. Ein Grund dafür ist, dass Dylan mit einem ganz eigenen Stil gesegnet ist - einem unvergleichlich dynamischen Stil!"

« Votre chroniqueur ne peut que reconnaître que ce disque semble être un des meilleurs que nous ait donné la bouillonnante scène folk depuis très, très longtemps... Dylan possède un style unique - un style individuel et dynamique ! »
VILLAGE VOICE, APRIL 26, 1962

MONDAY, MARCH 19, 1962

The debut album, **Bob Dylan**, is released in the United States. Initially poor sales—a reported 5,000 in the first year—will lead the record to be known around Columbia Records as "Hammond's Folly." The rockabilly-styled *Mixed-Up Confusion*, backed with *Corrina Corrina*, will be released as a single later in the year.

Das Debütalbum, **Bob Dylan**, kommt in den USA heraus. Die anfänglich miserablen Vorkaufszahlen, 5000 Stück im ersten Jahr, führen dazu, dass die Scheibe bei Columbia Records als „Hammonds Narretei" bezeichnet wird. *Mixed-Up Confusion* im Rockabilly-Stil erscheint mit *Corrina Corrina* auf der B-Seite später im Jahr als Single.

Le premier album, **Bob Dylan**, sort aux États-Unis. Les ventes commencent si doucement – quelque 5 000 exemplaires la première année – que le disque est rapidement surnommé chez Columbia « La folie de Hammond ». Quelques mois plus tard, le très rockabilly *Mixed-Up Confusion* sort en 45 tours, avec *Corrina Corrina* sur la face B.

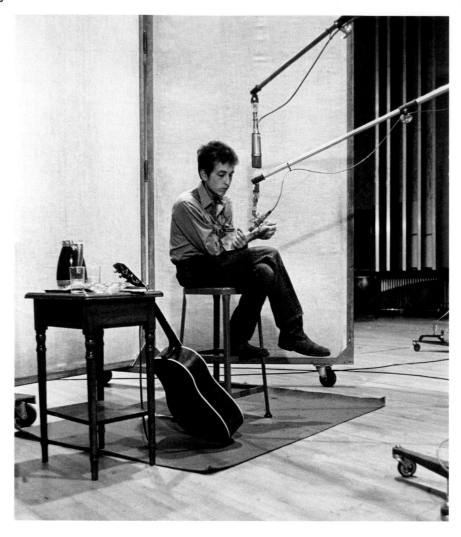

TUESDAY, APRIL 24, 1962

Returning to Columbia Records' Studio A, he cuts seven tracks. He will continue tomorrow, and intermittently through the rest of the year, completing the recording of his sophomore album, *The Freewheelin' Bob Dylan*.

Er kehrt ins Studio A der Columbia Records zurück und nimmt sieben neue Stücke auf. Am nächsten Tag macht er weiter und vollendet im Laufe des Jahres die Aufnahmen zu seinem zweiten Album *The Freewheelin' Bob Dylan*.

Dylan regagne le studio A de Columbia et enregistre sept chansons. Il continue le lendemain, puis par intermittence tout au long de l'année, jusqu'à achever son deuxième opus, *The Freewheelin' Bob Dylan*.

SATURDAY, SEPTEMBER 22, 1962
Sing Out! magazine's annual "Hootenanny" concert
takes place at New York's Carnegie Hall. Introduced
by Pete Seeger, Dylan sings *Sally Gal, Highway 51,
Talkin' John Birch Paranoid Blues, The Ballad Of Hollis
Brown,* and *A Hard Rain's A-Gonna Fall* before a
capacity crowd.
Das alljährliche „Hootenanny"-Konzert der Zeit-
schrift **Sing Out!** findet in der Carnegie Hall statt.
Dylan wird von Pete Seeger vorgestellt und singt vor
vollem Haus *Sally Gal, Highway 51, Talkin' John Birch
Paranoid Blues, The Ballad Of Hollis Brown* und
A Hard Rain's A-Gonna Fall.
Le *hootenanny* annuel du magazine **Sing Out!** a lieu
au Carnegie Hall, à New York. Présenté par Pete See-
ger, Dylan chante *Sally Gal, Highway 51, Talkin' John
Birch Paranoid Blues, The Ballad Of Hollis Brown* et
A Hard Rain's A-Gonna Fall devant une salle comble.

FRIDAY, OCTOBER 5, 1962
Joins John Lee Hooker, Ian & Sylvia, Judy Collins,
and others for the "Traveling Hootenanny" at New
York's Town Hall. An ad for the show reads: "Members
of the audience will be selected to perform! Bring your
guitars and banjos."
Auftritt mit John Lee Hooker, Ian & Sylvia, Judy Collins und anderen bei der Show „Traveling Hootenanny"
in der New Yorker Town Hall. In der Ankündigung
steht: „Ausgewählte Zuschauer dürfen mitspielen!
Bringen Sie Gitarre und Banjo mit."
Il se joint à John Lee Hooker, Ian & Sylvia, Judy
Collins et d'autres pour le *hootenanny* itinérant organisé au Town Hall de New York. Sur un prospectus
annonçant le spectacle, on peut lire : « Des membres
du public seront sélectionnés pour monter sur scène !
Apportez vos guitares et vos banjos. »

*"The depth and imagination of this 21-year-old's ragamuffin
minstrel's songs continue to amaze this listener."*
*„Der Tiefgang und die Fantasie in den Minstrel Songs dieses
21-jährigen Bengels verblüffen den Rezensenten immer wieder."*
*« La profondeur et l'imagination des chansons de ce
ménestrel raggamuffin de 21 ans ébahissent toujours celui qui
les écoute. »*
ROBERT SHELTON, THE NEW YORK TIMES

SATURDAY, DECEMBER 22, 1962

During his first visit to London, Dylan performs several shows in low-key venues, including tonight's at the Singers' Club Christmas Party at the Pindar of Wakefield pub in Grays Inn Road.

Bei seiner ersten London-Reise hat Dylan mehrere Auftritte an kleinen Veranstaltungsorten, so auch an diesem Abend bei der Singers' Club Christmas Party im Pindar of Wakefield Pub an der Grays Inn Road.

Lors de son premier séjour à Londres, Dylan se produit dans plusieurs petits clubs, notamment à la Fête de Noël du Singers' Club qui se tient au pub Pindar of Wakefield, sur Grays Inn Road.

SUNDAY, DECEMBER 30, 1962

Portraying a singing hobo, he performs *Swan On The River*, *Blowin' In The Wind*, *Hang Me*, and *Cuckoo Bird* on BBC-TV's play "The Madhouse On Castle Street," starring Ursula Howells, Maureen Pryor, and David Warner. The program will air on January 13, 1963.

Im BBC-Fernsehfilm „The Madhouse On Castle Street" mit Ursula Howells, Maureen Pryor und David Warner in den Hauptrollen spielt er einen singenden Landstreicher und gibt *Swan On The River*, *Blowin' In The Wind*, *Hang Me* und *Cuckoo Bird* zum Besten. Der Film wird am 13. Januar 1963 ausgestrahlt.

Costumé en chanteur vagabond, il chante *Swan On The River*, *Blowin' In The Wind*, *Hang Me* et *Cuckoo Bird* dans « The Madhouse On Castle Street », un téléfilm qui sera diffusé le 13 janvier 1963 sur la BBC, avec Ursula Howells, Maureen Pryor et David Warner.

FRIDAY, APRIL 12, 1963

Bob Dylan performs his first major, critically-praised solo concert at New York's Town Hall; it is recorded (though never released) by Columbia Records.

Bob Dylan hat sein erstes richtiges, von der Kritik gelobtes Solokonzert in der Town Hall in New York;

es wird von Columbia Records aufgezeichnet, aber nie veröffentlicht.

Bob Dylan donne son premier concert majeur en solo au Town Hall de New York. Loué par la critique, il est enregistré par Columbia Records, qui ne le diffusera jamais.

"A memorable evening of new songs by an incredibly gifted songwriter."

„Ein erinnerungswürdiger Abend mit neuen Liedern von einem ungemein begabten Songwriter."

« Une mémorable soirée de chansons nouvelles interprétées par un auteur-compositeur incroyablement doué. »

THE NEW YORK TIMES, APRIL 13, 1963

SUNDAY, MAY 12, 1963

Scheduled to perform *Talkin' John Birch Society Blues* on tonight's "The Ed Sullivan Show," on a bill topped by Vivien Leigh, he is asked during rehearsals by CBS Television executives to play a different song due to the song's wry attacks on segregation and the military. He declines. Sullivan and producer Bob Precht both oppose the network's decision.

Geplanter Auftritt mit *Talkin' John Birch Society Blues* bei der an diesem Tag ausgestrahlten „The Ed Sullivan Show", in der auch Vivien Leigh auftritt, er wird aber bei den Proben von den CBS-Fernsehchefs aufgefordert, ein anderes Stück zu spielen, das keine

Angriffe auf Rassentrennung und Militär enthält, was Dylan aber ablehnt. Sullivan und Produzent Bob Precht sind ebenfalls gegen die Entscheidung des Senders.

Alors qu'il doit interpréter *Talkin' John Birch Society Blues* dans l'émission du soir « The Ed Sullivan Show », avec Vivien Leigh comme invitée d'honneur, les patrons de CBS lui demandent, pendant les répétitions, de jouer un autre titre, en raison des attaques au vitriol contre la ségrégation et l'armée que contient la chanson. Il refuse. Sullivan et le producteur Bob Precht s'opposent tous deux à la décision de la chaîne.

SATURDAY, MAY 18, 1963

Having met her briefly at a party in Boston, Massachusetts, last year, he meets Joan Baez again, at the Monterey Folk Festival in Monterey, California, at which they both perform.

Dylan trifft Joan Baez wieder, nachdem er sie im Vorjahr kurz bei einer Party in Boston, Massachusetts, kennengelernt hat. Beide treten beim Monterey Folk Festival in Monterey, Kalifornien, auf.

Au Festival folk de Monterey (Californie), où ils se produisent tous les deux, Dylan retrouve Joan Baez, qu'il avait croisée un an plus tôt lors d'une fête à Boston (Massachusetts).

"Dylan is the stuff of which legends are made.
At 21 singing his own compositions, Dylan turns out to be not just an individual; he is an absolute original ... The prediction here is that his talent will be around for a long time."
„Dylan hat das Zeug zur Legende.
Mit 21 Jahren singt er seine eigenen Kompositionen, die nicht nur individuell, sondern absolut originell sind ... Unsere Voraussage ist, dass sein Talent lange vorhalten wird."
« Dylan est fait du même bois que les légendes.
À seulement 21 ans, il chante ses propres compositions et se révèle être bien plus qu'un simple individu; il est un original absolu... Je fais ici la prédiction que son talent ne va pas nous déserter avant longtemps. »
BILLBOARD, APRIL 27, 1963

MONDAY, MAY 27, 1963

The Freewheelin' Bob Dylan is released, featuring major compositions of his own, including *A Hard Rain's A-Gonna Fall, Blowin' In The Wind,* and *Masters Of War.* It establishes him as a leader in the burgeoning folk-singer-songwriter and youth-protest movements.

The Freewheelin' Bob Dylan kommt heraus, mit vielen wichtigen Kompositionen wie *A Hard Rain's A-Gonna Fall, Blowin' In The Wind* und *Masters Of War.* Damit etabliert er sich als Leitfigur in der entstehenden Singer-Songwriter-Folkszene und Jugend-Protestbewegung.

Sortie de *The Freewheelin' Bob Dylan,* qui comprend des compositions personnelles majeures comme *A Hard Rain's A-Gonna Fall, Blowin' In The Wind* et *Masters Of War.* Cet album fait de lui une icône de la génération montante de la jeunesse contestataire et une figure de proue de la scène folk.

SATURDAY, JULY 6, 1963

He sings *Only A Pawn In Their Game* at a voter-registration rally in Greenwood, Missisippi, with Pete Seeger, Theodore Bikel, and Josh White. He closes the show singing *We Shall Overcome* with Seeger.

Auftritt mit *Only A Pawn In Their Game* bei einer Wählerregistrierungskampagne in Greenwood, Missisippi, mit Pete Seeger, Theodore Bikel und Josh White. Als letztes Lied singt er zusammen mit Seeger *We Shall Overcome.*

Il chante *Only A Pawn In Their Game* lors d'un concert organisé à Greenwood (Mississippi) pour encourager la population à prendre leur carte d'électeur ; y participent également Pete Seeger, Theodore Bikel et Josh White. Il clôt le spectacle par un duo avec Seeger sur *We Shall Overcome.*

FRIDAY, JULY 26, 1963

The first day of the three-day Newport Folk Festival at Freebody Park in Newport, Rhode Island. He closes his set with *We Shall Overcome*, backed by a chorus comprising Peter, Paul, and Mary, Joan Baez, Theodore Bikel, Pete Seeger, and The Freedom Singers. He also duets with Baez to a workshop crowd.

Der erste Tag des dreitägigen Newport Folk Festival im Freebody Park in Newport, Rhode Island. Dylan beschließt seinen Auftritt mit *We Shall Overcome* unterstützt von einem Chor aus Peter, Paul and Mary, Joan Baez, Theodore Bikel, Pete Seeger und den Freedom Singers. Bei einem Workshop singt er im Duett mit Joan Baez.

Première journée du Festival folk de Newport (Rhode Island), qui se déroule sur trois jours au Freebody Park. Il conclut son set par une interprétation de *We Shall Overcome*, avec un chœur composé de Peter, Paul and Mary, Joan Baez, Theodore Bikel, Pete Seeger et des Freedom Singers. Il chante également en duo avec Joan Baez.

WEDNESDAY, AUGUST 28, 1963

Dylan performs at the end of an historic march on Washington at the Lincoln Memorial. Speaking from the steps of the memorial to a throng of more than 200,000 people who have marched for jobs, justice, and peace, the Reverend Martin Luther King Jr. delivers an emotionally charged speech that includes the refrain "I have a dream ... "

Dylan tritt am Ende des historischen Marschs auf Washington am Lincoln Memorial auf. Martin Luther King spricht vor dem Memorial zu über 200.000

Menschen, die für Arbeit, Gerechtigkeit und Frieden demonstrieren. In seiner aufrüttelnden Rede sagt er die berühmten Worte: „I have a dream ..."

Dylan se produit à l'issue de la marche historique sur Washington, au Mémorial Lincoln. Devant une

foule de plus de 200 000 personnes venues manifester pour des emplois, la justice et la paix, le révérend Martin Luther King prononce du haut des marches son émouvant discours au refrain devenu célèbre : « I have a dream... »

SATURDAY, OCTOBER 26, 1963
In the middle of recording tracks for his new album, Dylan performs at New York's Carnegie Hall. In attendance are his parents.
Während der Aufnahmen für sein neues Album spielt Dylan in der New Yorker Carnegie Hall. Im Publikum sitzen auch seine Eltern.
Alors qu'il est en plein enregistrement de son nouvel album, Dylan joue au Carnegie Hall de New York. Ses parents sont dans le public.

FRIDAY, DECEMBER 13, 1963
Dylan receives the Thomas Paine Award at the National Emergency Civil Liberties Committee's annual Bill of Rights dinner at New York's Americana Hotel.
Dylan nimmt den Thomas Paine Award beim alljährlichen Bill of Rights-Galadinner des National Emergency Civil Liberties Committee im New Yorker Americana Hotel entgegen.
Dylan reçoit le Prix Thomas Paine lors du gala annuel « Bill of Rights » donné par le Comité national pour les libertés civiles, à l'hôtel Americana de New York.

"There's no black and white, left and right to me anymore.
There's only up and down, and down is very close to the ground."
„Es gibt kein Schwarz und Weiß, kein links und rechts mehr für mich.
Es gibt nur oben und unten, und unten ist sehr nah am Boden."
« Pour moi, il n'y a plus ni noir, ni blanc, ni gauche, ni droite.
Il n'y a plus que en haut et en bas, et quand on est en bas, on est très près du sol. »
BOB DYLAN, DECEMBER 13, 1963

MONDAY, JANUARY 13, 1964
The Times They Are A-Changin' is released. With producer Tom Wilson solely at the helm, the record is the first to feature all self-penned material, and a return to his debut album, with Dylan accompanying himself on guitar and harmonica.
The Times They Are A-Changin' wird veröffentlicht. Tom Wilson ist der Produzent dieses ersten Albums, das ausschließlich selbst geschriebene Stücke enthält, bei denen Dylan sich auf Gitarre und Mundharmonika selbst begleitet.
Sortie de *The Times They Are A-Changin'*. Avec le producteur Tom Wilson seul à la barre, l'album est le premier à ne comporter que des titres originaux ; comme dans son premier album, Dylan s'accompagne à la guitare et à l'harmonica.

SUNDAY, MAY 17, 1964
Following an appearance on BBC TV's "Tonight" earlier in the week, Dylan makes his formal British concert debut at the Royal Festival Hall.
Nach einem Fernsehauftritt in der BBC-Sendung „Tonight" in der selben Woche gibt Dylan sein erstes richtiges Konzert in England in der Royal Festival Hall.
Après une apparition dans l'émission « Tonight », sur la BBC la semaine précédente, Dylan donne son premier concert officiel en Grande-Bretagne, au Royal Festival Hall.

TUESDAY, JUNE 9, 1964

Tracks for his forthcoming album, **Another Side Of Bob Dylan**, are recorded in a single three-hour session at Columbia Studios in New York. It is his only recording of the year.

Die Titel seines nächsten Albums, **Another Side Of Bob Dylan**, werden innerhalb von nur drei Stunden in den Columbia Studios in New York aufgenommen. Es ist sein einziger Studiotermin in diesem Jahr.

Il enregistre plusieurs titres de son futur album, **Another Side Of Bob Dylan**, lors d'une unique séance de trois heures aux studios de Columbia à New York. Il ne retournera pas en studio cette année-là.

SATURDAY, AUGUST 8, 1964

Dylan joins Joan Baez onstage at her performance in the Forest Hills Music Festival, at the Forest Hills Tennis Stadium in Queens, New York, duetting on his *With God On Our Side*. **New York Times** critic Robert Shelton, so unequivocal in his praise of Dylan in a 1961 article, is disappointed in Dylan's solo performance "with the lack of control of his stage manner, his raucously grating singing, and the somewhat declining level of his new composition."

Dylan kommt beim Forest Hills Music Festival zu Joan Baez auf die Bühne im Forest Hills Tennisstadion in Queens, New York, und singt mit ihr zusammen *With God On Our Side*. Robert Shelton, der Kritiker der **New York Times**, der Dylan 1961 so vorbehaltlos gefeiert hatte, ist über „sein unkontrolliertes Verhalten auf der Bühne, seinen heiser krächzenden Gesang und das nachlassende Niveau seiner neuen Kompositionen" enttäuscht.

Dylan rejoint Joan Baez sur scène lors du festival de musique de Forest Hills, dans le Queens (New York), pour un duo sur *With God On Our Side*. Le critique du **New York Times** Robert Shelton, si élogieux dans son article de 1961 sur Dylan, se dit déçu, cette fois, par « son manque de maîtrise dans son attitude sur scène, sa voix rauque et grinçante et le niveau déclinant de ses compositions ».

BOB DYLAN

AT PHILHARMONIC HALL

ONLY NEW YORK CONCERT APPEARANCE
ON SATURDAY OCTOBER 31ST AT 8:30PM

ALL SEATS RESERVED: $4.50, 4.00, 3.50, 2.75
ON SALE NOW AT PHILHARMONIC BOX OFFICE
Mail Orders To Philharmonic Hall, B'way at 65 St N.Y. 10023
ENCLOSE STAMPED SELF - ADDRESSED ENVELOPE

COLUMBIA RECORDS

"His developing control of those gifts and his ability to shape a meaningful program added up to a frequently spellbinding evening by the brilliant singing poet laureate of young America."
„Die wachsende Kontrolle über sein Talent und die Fähigkeit, ein aussagekräftiges Programm zusammenzustellen, trugen zu einem faszinierenden Abend mit dem singenden Dichterfürsten des jungen Amerika bei."
« Grâce à la maîtrise de son talent, en amélioration constante, et à sa capacité à façonner un programme riche, le poète chanteur prodige de la jeunesse américaine nous a fait passer une soirée souvent envoûtante. »
THE NEW YORK TIMES, NOVEMBER 2, 1964

SATURDAY, OCTOBER 31, 1964

Dylan plays to a sold-out crowd at New York's Philharmonic Hall. He is joined by Joan Baez on *Mama, You've Been On My Mind, Silver Dagger, With God On Our Side* and *It Ain't Me Babe*.

Dylan spielt in der ausverkauften New Yorker Philharmonic Hall. Bei *Mama, You've Been On My Mind, Silver Dagger, With God On Our Side* und *It Ain't Me Babe* wird er von Joan Baez begleitet.

Dylan se produit au Philharmonic Hall de New York devant une salle pleine à craquer. Joan Baez le rejoint sur scène pour chanter *Mama, You've Been On My Mind, Silver Dagger, With God On Our Side* et *It Ain't Me Babe*.

WEDNESDAY, JANUARY 13, 1965

Dylan begins the first of three recording sessions for his forthcoming LP, *Bringing It All Back Home*, at Columbia's Studio A in New York. Once again produced by Tom Wilson, this album features some career-defining songs, including *Maggie's Farm, Subterranean Homesick Blues, She Belongs To Me, Love Minus Zero/No Limit, Mr. Tambourine Man*, and *It's All Over Now, Baby Blue*. The album will top the

charts in the United Kingdom in May, and hit number 6 in the United States in October.

Dylan beginnt mit der ersten von drei Aufnahmesessions für seine nächste LP, *Bringing It All Back Home*, im Columbia Studio A in New York. Wieder ist Tom Wilson der Produzent des Albums, das eine ganze Reihe von Songs enthält, die Dylans Karriere prägen werden: *Maggie's Farm, Subterranean Homesick Blues, She Belongs To Me, Love Minus Zero/No Limit, Mr. Tambourine Man* und *It's All Over Now, Baby Blue*. Das Album steht im Mai an der Spitze der britischen Charts und erreicht in den USA im Oktober den 6. Platz.

Dylan entame la première d'une série de trois séances d'enregistrement pour son prochain album, *Bringing It All Back Home*, au Studio A de Columbia, à New York. Produit par Tom Wilson, ce 33 tours inclut certains des titres qui le rendront célèbre : *Maggie's Farm, Subterranean Homesick Blues, She Belongs To Me, Love Minus Zero/No Limit, Mr. Tambourine Man* et *It's All Over Now, Baby Blue*. L'album atteint la 1ᵉ place au Royaume-Uni en mai, puis, en octobre, la 6ᵉ place du classement américain.

FRIDAY, MARCH 26, 1965

Currently playing a residency at Los Angeles club Ciro's, The Byrds—who recorded Dylan's *Mr. Tambourine Man* in January—are joined onstage by the songwriter. The group will hit number one in both the United States and the UK with their folk-rock cover in the summer. It is the first chart-topping Dylan composition and sparks several pop and folk-rock hit covers of his material by major acts, including The Turtles (*It Ain't Me Babe*), Cher (*All I Really Want To Do*), Joan Baez (*It's All Over Now, Baby Blue* and *Farewell Angelina*), and Manfred Mann (*If You Gotta Go, Go Now*). At one point in the summer, his songs will be featured on 16 singles and 28 albums by other artists.

Die Byrds, die Dylans *Mr. Tambourine Man* im Januar aufgenommen haben, treten regelmäßig im Club Ciro in Los Angeles auf, wo der Verfasser des Songs zu ihnen auf die Bühne kommt. Mit ihrer Folkrock-Coverversion landet die Band im Sommer in den USA und England auf Platz 1. Es ist die erste Dylan-Komposition an der Spitze der Charts, und in

der Folge werden zahlreiche seiner Stücke in Pop- und Folkrockversionen gecovert, u. a. von den Turtles (*It Ain't Me Babe*), Cher (*All I Really Want To Do*), Joan Baez (*It's All Over Now, Baby Blue"* und Farewell Angelina") und Manfred Mann (*If You Gotta Go, Go Now*). In diesem Sommer sind seine Songs auf 16 Singles und 28 LPs anderer Künstler zu hören.

Dylan rejoint sur scène les Byrds, qui ont repris *Mr. Tambourine Man* en janvier et sont en résidence au club Ciro's, à Los Angeles. Pendant l'été, le groupe atteint le sommet des ventes aux États-Unis et au Royaume-Uni avec sa reprise folk-rock du titre, qui devient ainsi la première composition de Dylan à prendre la tête des classements. Il inaugure une longue série de reprises pop ou rock par des artistes reconnus comme les Turtles (*It Ain't Me Babe*), Cher (*All I Really Want To Do*), Joan Baez (*It's All Over Now, Baby Blue* et Farewell Angelina), ou Manfred Mann (*If You Gotta Go, Go Now*). Au cours du même été, ses chansons apparaîtront sur seize 45 tours et 28 albums d'autres artistes.

SATURDAY, MAY 8, 1965

With Dylan's every move on his United Kingdom trip caught on film by director D. A. Pennebaker for a forthcoming cinema verité release, "Don't Look Back," the singer-songwriter makes a promotional clip for his current single, *Subterranean Homesick Blues*. Standing in a scaffolding-filled alleyway next to the Savoy Hotel in London, a virtually motionless Dylan flicks through themed cards that contain pertinent short words and phrases, effectively creating one of the first music videos. The cards have been written by Joan Baez and The Animals' keyboardist, Alan Price. Actors Allen Ginsberg and Bob Neuwirth can be seen in the background. Pennebaker's fly-on-the-wall documentary follows the singer through jam sessions in hotels, confrontations with fans and journalists, limo rides, and stage performances.

Bei Dylans Englandtournee folgt ihm der Filmregisseur D. A. Pennebaker auf Schritt und Tritt mit der Kamera für seinen Dokufilm „Don't Look Back". Für seine aktuelle Single *Subterranean Homesick Blues* wird ein Werbe-Clip gedreht, der als Vorläufer des Musikvideos gilt. Dylan steht praktisch bewegungslos in einer Gasse am Savoy Hotel in London neben einem großen Baugerüst und durchblättert Papptafeln mit den wichtigsten Stichworten des Liedes. Die Tafeln wurden von Joan Baez und dem Keyboardspieler der Animals Alan Price geschrieben, im Hintergrund sind Allen Ginsberg und Bob Neuwirth zu sehen. In Pennebakers Dokumentarfilm ist der Sänger bei Jam Sessions in Hotels, bei Begegnungen mit Fans und Journalisten, bei Limofahrten und Auftritten zu sehen.

Pendant son voyage au Royaume-Uni, Dylan est suivi jour et nuit par le réalisateur D. A. Pennebaker, lequel prépare un documentaire pour le cinéma intitulé « Don't Look Back ». L'auteur-compositeur en profite pour tourner un petit film promotionnel pour son prochain 45 tours, *Subterranean Homesick Blues*. Debout dans une ruelle encombrée d'échafaudages, près de l'hôtel Savoy à Londres, un Dylan presque immobile présente les uns après les autres des cartons sur lesquels sont inscrits des groupes de mots tirés des paroles : il réalise ainsi le premier « clip » musical. Les pancartes ont été fabriquées par Joan Baez et le clavier des Animals, Alan Price ; on distingue Allen Ginsberg et Bob Neuwirth à l'arrière-plan. Le documentaire de Pennebaker montre les bœufs improvisés dans les hôtels, les rencontres avec les fans et les journalistes, les balades en limousine et les concerts.

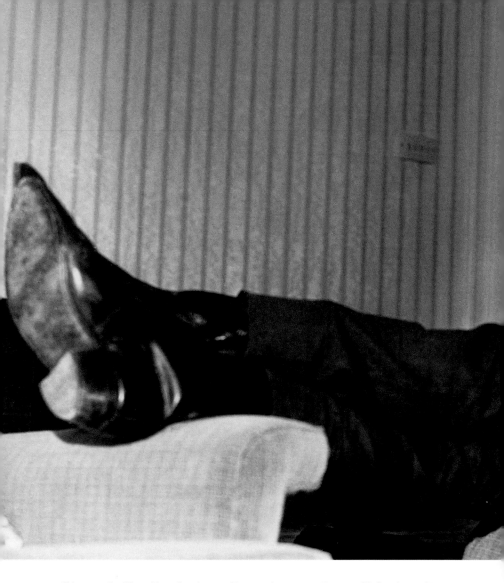

"I have six Cadillacs. I have four houses. I have a plantation in Georgia. Oh, I'm also working on a rocket. A little rocket. Not a big rocket. Not the kind of rocket they have in Cape Canaveral. I don't know about those kinds of rockets."

„Ich habe sechs Cadillacs. Ich habe vier Häuser. Ich habe eine Plantage in Georgia. Außerdem baue ich noch eine Rakete. Eine kleine Rakete. Keine große Rakete. Nicht so eine wie in Cape Canaveral. Mit der Art von Raketen kenne ich mich nicht aus."

« J'ai six Cadillac. J'ai quatre maisons. J'ai une plantation en Géorgie. Oh, je travaille aussi sur une fusée. Une petite fusée. Pas une grande. Pas le genre de fusée qu'ils ont à Cap Canaveral. Je ne connais rien à ces fusées-là. »
BOB DYLAN

MONDAY, MAY 10, 1965
Dylan finishes his United Kingdom tour with a performance at London's Royal Albert Hall.

Dylan schließt seine Englandtournee mit einem Auftritt in der Royal Albert Hall in London ab.

Dylan achève sa tournée britannique par un concert au Royal Albert Hall de Londres.

TUESDAY, JUNE 15, 1965

Five months after laying down tracks for his ***Bringing It All Back Home*** LP, Dylan returns to Columbia Studios to record material for ***Highway 61 Revisited***, his first entirely electric recording. He is accompanied by guitarists Mike Bloomfield and Al Gorgoni, bassist Joseph Macho, pianist Frank Owens, Bobby Gregg on drums, and Al Kooper—whose rolling Hammond organ part on *Like A Rolling Stone* will become one of rock music's most recognizable sounds.

Fünf Monate, nachdem er die Titel der LP ***Bringing It All Back Home*** eingespielt hat, kehrt Dylan ins Columbia Studio zurück, um die Aufnahmen für sein erstes vollständig elektronisches Album **Highway 61 Revisited** zu machen. Er wird von den Gitarristen Mike Bloomfield und Al Gorgoni, Bassist Joseph Macho, Pianist Frank Owens, Bobby Gregg am Schlagzeug und Al Kooper begleitet, dessen charakteristischer Hammondorgelpart in *Like A Rolling Stone* zu einem der bekanntesten Sounds der Rockmusik werden wird.

Cinq mois après avoir terminé son album **Bringing It All Back Home**, Dylan retourne aux studios de Columbia pour **Highway 61 Revisited**, son premier enregistrement entièrement électrique. Il est accompagné par les guitaristes Mike Bloomfield et Al Gorgoni, par le bassiste Joseph Macho, le pianiste Frank Owens, Bobby Gregg à la batterie et Al Kooper - dont la partie à l'orgue Hammond dans *Like A Rolling Stone* deviendra un des sons les plus reconnaissables de l'histoire du rock.

"A study in composing on several levels that raises the standard of folk and pop writing to new heights."
„Eine Vielschichtigkeit der Komposition, die die Folk- und Popmusik auf ein ganz neues Niveau hebt."
« Une composition travaillée sur plusieurs niveaux qui élève l'écriture folk et pop vers de nouveaux sommets. »
ROBERT SHELTON, THE NEW YORK TIMES

SUNDAY, JULY 25, 1965

Following an acoustic performance of *Mr. Tambourine Man* and *All I Really Want To Do* at yesterday's afternoon workshop, Dylan plays his first electric set at the Newport Folk Festival, backed by Al Kooper and Barry Goldberg on organ and the Paul Butterfield Blues Band rhythm section of Mike Bloomfield, Jerome Arnold, and Sam Lay. Over the years, opinions will vary as to what happened next. Most media reports will allege that die-hard acoustic-folk "purists" in the audience tried to boo him off stage, while some firsthand accounts claim that Dylan's electric experimentation was met by an enthusiastic response. Meanwhile, Dylan is creatively restless and keen to broaden his musical spectrum, a decision that will engender long-term respect and commercial return.

Nach einer akustischen Performance beim Workshop am Vortag spielt Dylan beim Newport Folk Festival sein erstes Konzert mit elektrisch verstärkten Instrumenten, unterstützt vom Al Kooper und Barry Goldberg an der Orgel und der Rhythmusgruppe der Paul Butterfield Blues Band, bestehend aus Mike Bloomfield, Jerome Arnold und Sam Lay. Im Laufe der Jahre gingen die Meinungen über das, was dann geschah, auseinander. Die meisten Medienberichte behaupten, dass die eingefleischten „Puristen" im

Publikum, für die Folkmusik akustisch zu sein hatte, ihn von der Bühne zu buhen versuchten. Anderen Berichten aus erster Hand zufolge stießen Dylans Experimente mit elektrischer Verstärkung auf begeisterte Zustimmung. Auf jeden Fall wurden Dylans rastlose Kreativität und sein unbedingter Wille, sein musikalisches Spektrum zu erweitern, offenbar – was ihm auf lange Sicht viel Respekt und auch kommerziellen Erfolg eintrug.

Dylan donne son premier concert électrique au Newport Folk Festival, avec Al Kooper et Barry Goldberg à l'orgue et la section rythmique du Paul Butterfield Blues Band, composée de Mike Bloomfield, Jerome Arnold et Sam Lay. Ce qui s'est passé ensuite a été raconté de différentes façons au fil des années. La plupart des articles de presse prétendent que les « puristes » inconditionnels du folk acoustique présents dans le public l'ont hué pour essayer de le sortir de scène, tandis que d'autres témoins directs assurent que les expérimentations électriques de Dylan ont été accueillies avec enthousiasme. Mais tous comprennent que la créativité de Dylan ne connaît pas de répit et qu'il cherche à élargir son spectre musical ; une volonté qui engendrera un respect et un succès commercial durables.

*"It's all music; no more, no less. I know in my own mind what I'm doing.
If anyone has imagination, he'll know what I'm doing. If they can't understand my
songs, they're missing something. If they can't understand green clocks, wet
chairs, purple lamps, or hostile status, they're missing something too."*

*„Es ist alles Musik, nicht mehr und nicht weniger. In meinem Kopf ist mir völlig
klar, was ich tue. Wenn jemand auch nur ein bisschen Fantasie hat, wird er
verstehen, was ich tue. Wer meine Lieder nicht versteht, hat irgendwas nicht
kapiert. Wer grüne Uhren, nasse Stühle, lila Lampen oder Feindstatus nicht
versteht, der hat ebenfalls irgendwas nicht kapiert."*

*« Tout ça, c'est de la musique ; rien de plus, rien de moins. Dans mon esprit, je
sais ce que je fais. Quiconque a de l'imagination comprend ce que je fais. S'ils
n'arrivent pas à comprendre mes chansons, ils manquent quelque chose. S'ils ne
comprennent pas les horloges vertes, les chaises mouillées, les lampes violettes
ou l'hostilité, ils passent à côté de quelque chose. »*

BOB DYLAN, AUGUST 27, 1965

SATURDAY, AUGUST 28, 1965

Dylan's fall tour begins at the Forest Hills Music Festival at the Forest Hills Tennis Stadium in Forest Hills, New York. At his first concert since the controversial Newport Folk Festival appearance, Dylan is introduced by the disk jockey Murray the K, who is roundly booed by some among the 15,000-strong audience. Dylan plays a solo set of seven numbers, opening with *She Belongs To Me* and ending with *Mr. Tambourine Man*, and then returns to the stage backed by keyboardist Al Kooper, bassist Harvey Brooks, and two members of The Hawks: 21-year-old Canadian Robbie Robertson on guitar, and 23-year-old Arizona native Levon Helm on drums. The second half is an eight-song set with *Maggie's Farm* and *Like A Rolling Stone* among its highlights. This format, an acoustic set followed by an electric one, is kept throughout the tour and during next year's world trek.

Der Auftakt zu Dylans Herbsttournee findet beim Forest Hills Music Festival in Forest Hills, New York, statt. Bei seinem ersten Konzert seit dem umstrittenen Auftritt beim Newport Folk Festival wird Dylan vom Diskjockey Murray the K angesagt, der von etlichen der 15.000 Zuschauer laut ausgebuht wird. Dylan spielt sieben Solostücke, *She Belongs To Me* zum Einstieg und *Mr. Tambourine Man* zum Abschluss; dann kehrt er mit Keyboarder Al Kooper, Bassist Harvey Brooks und zwei Mitgliedern der Band The Hawks auf die Bühne zurück: mit dem 21 jährigen Kanadier Robbie Robertson an der Gitarre und dem 23-jährigen Levon Helm aus Arizona an den Drums. In der zweiten Hälfte werden acht Songs gespielt, von denen *Maggie's Farm* und *Like A Rolling Stone* zu den Highlights gehören. Dieses Format, bei dem eine elektrische auf eine akustische Setlist folgt, wird auf der gesamten Tournee durch die USA und die Welt in diesem und dem nächsten Jahr beibehalten.

La tournée automnale de Dylan débute par le festival de Forest Hills (New York). Pour cette première apparition sur scène depuis son concert controversé du Newport Folk Festival, Dylan est présenté par le disque-jockey Murray the K, copieusement hué par une partie des quelque 15 000 spectateurs présents. Dylan joue sept morceaux seul : il commence par *She Belongs To Me* et termine avec *Mr. Tambourine Man* ; il revient ensuite, accompagné de l'organiste Al Kooper, du bassiste Harvey Brooks et de deux membres des Hawks – le Canadien de 21 ans Robbie Robertson à la guitare et Levon Helm, 23 ans, originaire d'Arizona, à la batterie – pour la deuxième partie de son set, composée de huit chansons, parmi lesquelles *Maggie's Farm* et *Like A Rolling Stone*. Cette configuration (une partie acoustique suivie d'une partie électrique) est conservée pour tout le reste de la tournée mondiale.

MONDAY, FEBRUARY 14, 1966

After six sessions in New York recording his new album, Dylan decamps to Columbia Music Row Studios in Nashville, Tennessee, where he is backed by the cream of current Nashville session musicians, including Charlie McCoy, Hargus "Pig" Robbins, Jerry Kennedy, Wayne Moss, and Kenny Buttrey.

Nach sechs Aufnahmesessions in New York zieht Dylan in die Columbia Music Row Studios in Nashville um, wo er von der Elite der Studiomusiker in Nashville bei den Aufnahmen zu seinem neuen Album unterstützt wird: Charlie McCoy, Hargus „Pig" Robbins, Jerry Kennedy, Wayne Moss und Kenny Buttrey.

Après six sessions à New York, Dylan part finir l'enregistrement de son album aux studios Music Row de Columbia à Nashville (Tennessee), en compagnie de la crème des musiciens de studio locaux, notamment Charlie McCoy, Hargus « Pig » Robbins, Jerry Kennedy, Wayne Moss et Kenny Buttrey.

TUESDAY, MAY 17, 1966

Following single concerts in Sweden, Denmark, and Ireland, and eight dates into the UK leg of his world tour, Dylan performs at the Free Trade Hall in Manchester—a concert that is illegally recorded and subsequently in demand as the most popular bootleg of all time (though it is incorrectly and mythically named The Royal Albert Hall Concert). Before performing *Like A Rolling Stone*, the final number of his second-half electric set, someone in the audience shouts "Judas," to which Dylan replies "I don't believe you" and turns to the band and instructs them to "play f***ing loud."

Nach jeweils einem Konzert in Schweden, Dänemark und Irland und acht Auftritten in England spielt Dylan auf seiner Welttournee in der Free Trade Hall in Manchester – ein Konzert, das illegal mitgeschnitten wird und sich später zum gefragtesten Bootleg aller Zeiten entwickelt (auch wenn es fälschlicherweise „The Royal Albert Hall Concert" genannt wird). Vor der Nummer *Like A Rolling Stone*, der letzten seiner elektrisch verstärkten Konzerthälfte, schreit jemand im Publikum „Judas", woraufhin Dylan antwortet: „Das glaube ich nicht", sich zur Band umdreht und sie auffordert: „Play fucking loud."

Après des concerts uniques en Suède, au Danemark et en Irlande et les huit premières dates de la partie britannique de sa tournée mondiale, Dylan se produit au Free Trade Hall de Manchester – la soirée est enregistrée illégalement et cette bande pirate devient la plus recherchée de tous les temps (bien qu'elle soit faussement appelée « The Royal Albert Hall Concert »). Avant qu'il commence *Like A Rolling Stone*, le dernier titre de son set électrique, quelqu'un dans le public crie : « Judas ! » Dylan réplique : « Je ne te crois pas », se tourne vers le groupe et leur donne la consigne d'« envoyer un p... de son. »

"There was a marked and disturbing contrast between the two parts of the concert given by Bob Dylan, the American folk singer, at the Albert Hall last night. In the first, and infinitely better, half of the evening, Mr. Dylan gave an agreeable solo rendering of some of the songs for which he is best known: in the second half he was accompanied by a thunderous quintet who made it virtually impossible to distinguish a single line of the lyrics ... Bob Dylan is often thought to speak, through his songs, for his generation; it seems all the more unfortunate that for one half of this entertainment the words should have been impossible to hear."

„Es gab einen deutlichen, beunruhigenden Kontrast zwischen den beiden Hälften des Konzerts, das gestern Abend von Bob Dylan, dem amerikanischen Folksänger, in der Albert Hall gegeben wurde. Während der ersten und unendlich viel besseren Hälfte des Abends gab Mr. Dylan eine angenehme Solodarbietung etlicher seiner bekanntesten Lieder. In der zweiten Hälfte wurde er von einem donnernden Quintett begleitet, das es im Grunde unmöglich machte, eine einzige Textzeile zu verstehen ... Es wird oft gesagt, dass Bob Dylan durch seine Songs für seine Generation spricht. Umso bedauerlicher scheint es, dass es bei einer Hälfte seines Konzerts unmöglich ist, etwas von den Worten zu verstehen."

« Il y avait un contraste marqué et dérangeant entre les deux parties du concert donné hier soir par Bob Dylan, le chanteur folk américain, à l'Albert Hall. Dans la première - et infiniment meilleure - partie de la soirée, M. Dylan a joliment interprété en solo certaines des chansons pour lesquelles il est le plus connu ; dans la seconde, il était accompagné d'un quintette tonitruant qui empêchait de distinguer le moindre mot... On pense souvent que Bob Dylan parle, à travers ses chansons, pour sa génération ; il semble d'autant plus regrettable que pendant la moitié de son numéro, les paroles aient été inaudibles. »

THE TIMES

FRIDAY, JULY 29, 1966

Dylan suffers injuries (never fully detailed, but apparently involving several broken vertebrae) when he crashes his Triumph 55 motorcycle near manager Albert Grossman's home in Bearsville, New York. He is apparently riding his bike to a garage for repairs when the rear wheel locks, throwing it out of control and hurling him over the handlebars. His recuperation, purportedly on Cape Cod, Massachusetts, leads to a period of reclusive inactivity, interpreted by many as an attempt to escape into family life, away from the extreme pressures of two years' success.

Dylan wird bei einem Motorradunfall in der Nähe des Hauses seines Managers Albert Grossman in Bearsville, New York, auf seiner Triumph 55 schwer verletzt (Details werden nie bekannt gegeben, aber es scheinen mehrere Wirbel gebrochen zu sein). Er will offenbar das Motorrad zur Reparatur in die Werkstatt bringen, als das Hinterrad blockiert, Dylan die Kontrolle verliert und über die Lenkstange fliegt. Seine Genesung, angeblich auf Cape Cod in Massachusetts, mündet in eine Phase des Rückzugs und der Untätigkeit, die von vielen als Versuch interpretiert wird, sich ins Familienleben zurückzuziehen, fort von dem übergroßen Druck der letzten zwei extrem erfolgreichen Jahre.

Dylan est blessé (on ignore les détails, si ce n'est qu'il semble avoir eu plusieurs vertèbres brisées) lors d'un accident avec sa Triumph 55 près de chez son agent Albert Grossman, à Bearsville (New York). Il conduisait apparemment sa moto au garage pour des réparations lorsque la roue arrière s'est bloquée ; il aurait alors perdu le contrôle de l'engin avant d'être propulsé par-dessus le guidon. Sa convalescence, qui se serait déroulée à Cape Cod (Massachusetts), est suivie d'une période d'isolement oisif, que beaucoup ont interprétée comme une tentative d'échapper aux pressions engendrées par ses deux années de succès en trouvant refuge dans la vie de famille.

© John Byrne Cooke, www.cookephoto.com

TUESDAY, APRIL 25, 1967

Columbia Records announces that a contract dispute with Dylan has been settled amicably. The singer had been suspended by the company for failing to make the required number of recordings. The contract requires Dylan to provide 14 new songs.

Columbia Records gibt bekannt, dass eine Vertragsstreitigkeit mit Dylan gütlich beigelegt worden sei. Der Sänger wurde vom Label suspendiert, weil er nicht die vertraglich festgelegte Anzahl von Platten aufgenommen hat; laut Vertrag muss er 14 neue Songs liefern.

Columbia Records annonce qu'un conflit portant sur le contrat de Dylan a été réglé à l'amiable avec l'artiste. Ce dernier avait été suspendu par la maison de disque pour ne pas lui avoir livré le nombre prévu d'albums. Par contrat, Dylan devait encore quatorze chansons à Columbia.

TUESDAY, OCTOBER 17, 1967

After spending the summer and early fall in seclusion with The Hawks (who subsequently became The Band) at a rented house in Saugerties, New York, where they recorded more than 50 tracks, later released as *The Basement Tapes*, Dylan returns to the studios at Columbia's Studio A in Nashville, where, backed by Charlie McCoy on bass and Kenny Buttrey on drums, he begins work on the *John Wesley Harding* sessions.

Nachdem er sich im Sommer und Frühherbst in völliger Zurückgezogenheit mit den Hawks (die dann später The Band wurden) in einem Haus in Saugerties, New York, eingemietet hat, wo sie über 50 Stücke aufgenommen haben, die später als *The Basement Tapes* veröffentlicht werden, kehrt Dylan ins Plattenstudio zurück. Im Columbia Studio A in Nashville beginnt er mit Charlie McCoy am Bass und Kenny Buttrey an den Drums mit den Aufnahmen zu *John Wesley Harding*.

Dylan a passé l'été et le début de l'automne reclus avec les Hawks (qui deviendront bientôt « The Band », le groupe) dans une maison louée à Saugerties (New York), où ils ont enregistré plus de cinquante titres, qui sortiront plus tard sous le nom de *The Basement Tapes*. Il reprend le chemin du Studio A de Columbia à Nashville, où, accompagné de Charlie McCoy à la basse et de Kenny Buttrey à la batterie, il commence les enregistrements de *John Wesley Harding*.

SATURDAY, JANUARY 20, 1968

Making his first public appearance since his motorcycle accident, Dylan, backed by The Hawks, takes part in the Woody Guthrie Memorial Concert held at Carnegie Hall. Pete Seeger, Arlo Guthrie, Odetta, Richie Havens, Judy Collins, and Ramblin' Jack Elliott also pay their musical respects to the iconic folk artist who passed away in October.

Bei seinem ersten öffentlichen Auftritt seit dem Unfall nimmt Dylan zusammen mit den Hawks am Woody Guthrie Memorial Concert in der Carnegie Hall teil. Auch Pete Seeger, Arlo Guthrie, Odetta, Richie Havens, Judy Collins und Ramblin' Jack Elliott erweisen der im Oktober verstorbenen Folk-Ikone die letzte Ehre.

Première apparition publique de Dylan depuis son accident de moto : avec les Hawks, il participe au concert à la mémoire de Woody Guthrie, au Carnegie Hall. Pete Seeger, Arlo Guthrie, Odetta, Richie Havens, Judy Collins et Ramblin' Jack Elliott rendent aussi hommage à cette grande figure de la musique folk, décédée en octobre.

MONDAY, FEBRUARY 17, 1969

Having already spent three days at Columbia's Studio A in Nashville cutting tracks for the upcoming *Nashville Skyline* album, Dylan is joined by Johnny Cash. The two record close to two dozen songs, although only one of their duet tracks will ever be issued—*Girl From The North Country*.

Nachdem Dylan bereits drei Tage lang neue Titel für das Album *Nashville Skyline* aufgenommen hat, kommt Johnny Cash zu ihm ins Columbia Studio A in Nashville. Die beiden nehmen fast zwei Dutzend Songs zusammen auf, aber nur ein einziges ihrer Duette wird je veröffentlicht: *Girl From The North Country*.

Dylan a déjà passé trois jours au Studio A de Nashville à mixer les titres du futur album *Nashville Skyline*, lorsqu'il est rejoint par Johnny Cash. Les deux musiciens enregistrent plus de vingt chansons, mais un seul de leurs duos sera publié : *Girl From The North Country*.

SATURDAY, JUNE 7, 1969

"The Johnny Cash Show" premieres on ABC Television, with Dylan guesting. Taped at The Ryman Auditorium in Nashville on May 1, Dylan sings *I Threw It All Away* and *Living The Blues* and duets with Cash on *Girl From The North Country*.

„The Johnny Cash Show" wird zum ersten Mal auf ABC Television ausgestrahlt, Dylan ist der erste Gaststar. Es werden Mitschnitte aus dem Ryman Auditorium in Nashville vom 1. Mai gezeigt – Dylan singt *I Threw It All Away* und *Living The Blues* und zusammen mit Cash *Girl From The North Country*.

Première diffusion du «Johnny Cash Show» sur la chaîne ABC, enregistré à l'auditorium Ryman de Nashville le 1er mai. Dylan, invité spécial, chante *I Threw It All Away* et *Living The Blues*, ainsi que *Girl From The North Country* en duo avec Cash.

*"Bob Dylan came here to do what he had to
do and he's done it, and I'm afraid that's the end."*
*„Bob Dylan ist hergekommen um zu tun, was er tun musste,
und er hat es getan, und ich fürchte, das ist das Ende."*
*«Bob Dylan est venu faire ce qu'il avait à faire,
il l'a fait, et j'ai bien peur que ce soit tout.»*
RIKKI FARR, PRODUCER OF THE ISLE OF WIGHT FESTIVAL

SUNDAY, AUGUST 31, 1969

After declining an invitation to perform at Wood-
stock, Dylan closes the second annual Isle of Wight
Festival at Woodside Bay in Godshill on the Isle of
Wight. Paying £3 for the four-day bash, more than
100,000 attendees show up to see him make his first
United Kingdom appearance in more than three years.
He is reportedly paid £35,000 for his 17-song, hour-
plus-long set.

Dylan lehnt die Teilnahme am Woodstock Festival
ab und spielt stattdessen als Höhepunkt des zweiten
Isle of Wight Festivals in Godshill auf der Kanalinsel
Isle of Wight. Über 100.000 Zuschauer kommen (zum
Eintrittspreis von 3 Pfund pro Person), um ihn bei
seinem ersten England-Gig seit über drei Jahren zu
sehen. Angeblich erhält er für seinen über eine Stunde
langen Auftritt mit 17 Stücken 35.000 Pfund.

Dylan a décliné la proposition de jouer à Woodstock,
et conclut le deuxième festival annuel de l'île de Wight,
sur la baie de Woodside, à Godshill. Le passe pour
quatre jours de concerts est vendu trois livres, et plus de
100 000 personnes viennent écouter le premier concert de Dylan sur le sol britannique en plus de trois ans.
Il aurait été payé 35 000 livres pour une grande heure
de présence sur scène, un set de dix-sept chansons.

THE 1970ˢ

DIE 1970ER

LES ANNÉES 1970

FRIDAY, MAY 1, 1970

Having only just completed sessions for what will be his *Self Portrait* album, Dylan returns to Columbia's Studio B in New York and spends the day jamming with George Harrison. This is not the first time Dylan and Harrison have collaborated. In November 1968, Harrison had spent some time at Dylan's Woodstock home, cutting *Nowhere To Go* and *I'd Have You Anytime*.

Dylan hat gerade erst die Aufnahmen für das Album *Self Portrait* abgeschlossen und kehrt zu einer Jam Session mit George Harrison ins Studio B der Columbia in New York zurück. Dylan und Harrison arbeiten nicht zum ersten Mal zusammen. Im November 1968 verbrachte Harrison einige Zeit bei Dylan zu Hause in Woodstock, wo die Titel *Nowhere To Go* und *I'd Have You Anytime* entstanden.

Alors qu'il vient d'achever l'enregistrement de ce qui deviendra l'album *Self Portrait*, Dylan retourne au Studio B de Columbia, à New York, où il passe la journée à jouer avec George Harrison. Déjà en novembre 1968, les deux hommes s'étaient retrouvés au domicile de Dylan, à Woodstock; de leur collaboration étaient nés *Nowhere To Go* et *I'd Have You Anytime*.

"Although he is reaching the perilous age of 30,
his music remains the authentic expression of the disturbed and
concerned conscience of young America."
*„Trau keinem über 30, so sagt man, doch die Musik, die Dylan
mit fast 30 macht, ist nach wie vor der authentische Ausdruck
des ruhelosen Gewissens des jungen Amerika."*
*« Bien qu'il approche de l'âge fatidique de trente ans,
sa musique demeure l'expression authentique de la conscience
perturbée et anxieuse de la jeunesse américaine. »*
PRINCETON UNIVERSITY CITATION

TUESDAY, JUNE 9, 1970
Dylan is awarded an honorary doctorate in music
from Princeton University in Princeton, New Jersey.
The proceedings are interrupted by an invasion of
cicadas, which he later writes about in the song *Day
Of The Locusts*. Martin Luther King Jr.'s widow,
Coretta Scott King, is also so honored.
Dylan wird von der Princeton University in Prince-
ton, New Jersey, zum Ehrendoktor der Musik ernannt.
Die Feierlichkeiten werden von einer Zikadeninvasion

unterbrochen, über die er später in dem Song *Day Of
The Locusts* schreibt. Martin Luther Kings Witwe,
Coretta Scott King, wird ebenfalls geehrt.
Dylan est nommé docteur honoris causa en
musique par l'université de Princeton (New Jersey).
La cérémonie est interrompue par une invasion de
cigales, à laquelle il fera référence dans sa chanson
Day Of The Locusts. La veuve de Martin Luther King,
Coretta Scott King, est honorée le même jour.

MONDAY, MAY 24, 1971

Dylan visits the Wailing Wall in Jerusalem on his 30th birthday. Later in the week he will visit the Givat Haim kibbutz with the thought of perhaps moving there with his family. Much to his alleged chagrin, his record label in Israel takes out an ad in **The Jerusalem Post** wishing him a happy birthday and asking him to get in touch.

An seinem 30. Geburtstag besucht Dylan die Klagemauer in Jerusalem. Später in derselben Woche stattet er dem Givat Haim Kibbuz einen Besuch ab, weil er darüber nachdenkt, mit seiner Familie dorthin zu ziehen. Zu seinem großen Ärger veröffentlicht seine Plattenfirma eine Anzeige in der **Jerusalem Post**, in der sie ihm zum Geburtstag gratuliert und ihn bittet sich zu melden.

Dylan se rend au mur des Lamentations, à Jérusalem, le jour de son trentième anniversaire. Plus tard dans la semaine, il visite le kibboutz de Givat Haim, où il envisage de s'installer avec sa famille. Pour son plus grand déplaisir, apparemment, la maison de disques qui le représente en Israël publie dans le **Jerusalem Post** un encart pour lui souhaiter un bon anniversaire et lui demander d'entrer en contact avec elle.

SUNDAY, AUGUST 1, 1971

After receiving a personal plea for help from his friend Ravi Shankar, George Harrison has organized "The Concert for Bangladesh" to aid victims of famine and war in Bangladesh. With two shows in one day at New York's Madison Square Garden, the lineup of artists includes Dylan, Eric Clapton, Billy Preston, Leon Russell, Ringo Starr, and Shankar, with musical backing from Badfinger, Jesse Ed Davis, Jim Horn, Jim Keltner, Don Nix, and Carl Radle. This is Dylan's only major live appearance of the year.

Auf das persönliche Hilfegesuch seines Freundes Ravi Shankar hin hat George Harrison das „Concert for Bangladesh" organisiert, zur Hilfe der Opfer von Krieg und Hungersnot in Bangladesch. Im New Yorker Madison Square Garden finden zwei Konzerte an einem Tag mit einem üppigen Aufgebot an Künstlern statt: Dylan, Eric Clapton, Billy Preston, Leon Russell, Ringo Starr und Shankar, mit musikalischer Unterstützung von Badfinger, Jesse Ed Davis, Jim Horn, Jim Keltner, Don Nix und Carl Radle. Es ist Dylans einziger größerer Auftritt in diesem Jahr.

Après avoir reçu l'appel au secours de son ami Ravi Shankar, George Harrison a organisé un « Concert pour le Bangladesh » pour rassembler des fonds à destination des victimes de la famine et de la guerre dans ce pays. De nombreux artistes participent aux deux concerts de la journée, au Madison Square Garden de New York : Dylan, Eric Clapton, Billy Preston, Leon Russell, Ringo Starr et Shankar, accompagnés de Badfinger, Jesse Ed Davis, Jim Horn, Jim Keltner, Don Nix et Carl Radle, entre autres. Il s'agit de la seule apparition majeure sur scène de Dylan cette année-là.

SATURDAY, JANUARY 1, 1972

Dylan appears unannounced at The Band's New Year's Eve concert at the Academy of Music in New York. He begins playing four songs about 15 minutes into the New Year.

Dylan erscheint unangekündigt beim Silvesterkonzert von The Band in der Academy of Music in New York. Ungefähr 15 Minuten nach Mitternacht fängt er mit seinen vier Stücken an.

Dylan fait une apparition surprise au concert du Nouvel An de The Band, à l'Academy of Music de New York. Il commence à jouer ses quatre chansons environ quinze minutes après les douze coups de minuit.

THURSDAY, NOVEMBER 23, 1972
Dylan arrives with his family in Durango, Mexico, to start filming his role as the outlaw Alias in Sam Peckinpah's cowboy movie "Pat Garrett And Billy The Kid"— for which he will also contribute three songs to the soundtrack album, including a new composition, *Knockin' On Heaven's Door*.

Dylan reist mit seiner Familie zu Dreharbeiten nach Durango, Mexiko; er spielt einen Outlaw in Sam Peckinpahs Western „Pat Garrett jagt Billy The Kid" – Dylan steuert auch drei Songs zum Soundtrack bei, darunter die neue Komposition *Knockin' On Heaven's Door*.

Dylan arrive avec sa famille à Durango, au Mexique, pour tourner le western de Sam Peckinpah «Pat Garrett et Billy The Kid», dans lequel il interprète le rôle du hors-la-loi Alias; il signe aussi trois chansons de la bande originale, dont *Knockin' On Heaven's Door*.

FRIDAY, NOVEMBER 2, 1973

Dylan begins six days of sessions at the Village Recorder studios in Santa Monica, California, backed on five tracks by Robbie Robertson and The Band. Dylan's label agreement with Columbia expired in September and he elected not to renew it, signing instead a one-off album deal with David Geffen's red-hot Asylum label. These sessions will be released as *Planet Waves* and ironically become his first United States chart-topping set.

Dylan beginnt eine sechstägige Aufnahmesession in den Village Recorder Studios in Santa Monica, Kalifornien, bei fünf Titeln wird er von Robbie Robertson und The Band begleitet. Dylans Plattenvertrag bei Columbia ist im September ausgelaufen, und er hat sich gegen eine Verlängerung entschieden und stattdessen einen Ein-Album-Vertrag mit David Geffens angesagtem Label Asylum unterschrieben. Die Aufnahmen werden unter dem Album-Titel *Planet Waves* veröffentlicht, ironischerweise seine erste Scheibe an der Spitze der US-Charts.

Dylan entame une session de six jours d'enregistrement aux studios Village Recorder de Santa Monica (Californie); sur cinq titres, il est accompagné de Robbie Robertson et de The Band. Dylan a choisi de ne pas renouveler son contrat avec Columbia, qui a expiré en septembre, préférant signer pour un seul album avec le tout nouveau label de David Geffen, Asylum. Ces sessions seront éditées sous le titre *Planet Waves* et deviendront le premier album de Dylan à atteindre le sommet des ventes aux États-Unis.

THURSDAY, JANUARY 3, 1974

Dylan and The Band—who also play their own standalone set—open a 40-date North America tour (Dylan's first in nearly eight years) at Chicago Stadium. More than 5 million applications have been received for the 660,000 tickets available.

Dylan und The Band – die an diesem Abend auch ein eigenes Set spielen – geben im Chicago Stadium den Auftakt zu einer Nordamerikatournee mit 40 Konzerten (Dylans erste Tour seit fast acht Jahren). Für die zur Verfügung stehenden 660.000 Karten gehen über 5 Millionen Gesuche ein.

Dylan et The Band – qui joue aussi sans Dylan ce soir-là – inaugurent une tournée de 40 dates en Amérique du Nord (la première de Dylan depuis près de huit ans) au Chicago Stadium. Plus de cinq millions de demandes arrivent pour 660 000 billets disponibles.

THURSDAY, MAY 9, 1974

Dylan takes part in the "Friends Of Chile" benefit concert at New York's Felt Forum, raising $30,000 toward legal-aid fees for Chilean refugees and political prisoners. He performs four songs with Arlo Guthrie, Melanie, Phil Ochs, Dave Van Ronk, and Pete Seeger.

Dylan nimmt an dem „Friends Of Chile"-Benefizkonzert im New Yorker Felt Forum teil, bei dem 30.000 Dollar zugunsten der Anwaltskosten für chilenische Flüchtlinge und politische Häftlinge zusammenkommen. Gemeinsam mit Arlo Guthrie, Melanie, Phil Ochs, Dave Van Ronk und Pete Seeger spielt er vier Titel.

Dylan participe au concert de charité « Les Amis du Chili » au Felt Forum de New York, qui permet de rassembler 30 000 dollars pour apporter une aide juridique aux réfugiés et prisonniers politiques chiliens. Il joue quatre chansons avec Arlo Guthrie, Melanie, Phil Ochs, Dave Van Ronk et Pete Seeger.

FRIDAY, AUGUST 2, 1974

Following the release of two albums on Asylum, Bob Dylan settles his differences with Columbia and re-signs to the label for five years. He will begin recording material for the **Blood On The Tracks** album on September 16.

Nach zwei Alben beim Asylum-Label legt Bob Dylan seine Meinungsverschiedenheiten mit Columbia Records bei und verpflichtet sich für die nächsten fünf Jahre dort. Am 16. September beginnt er mit dem Einspielen von Material für die LP **Blood On The Tracks**.

Après deux albums chez Asylum, Bob Dylan règle son différend avec Columbia et signe un nouveau contrat de cinq ans. Il commence à enregistrer la matière de **Blood On The Tracks** le 16 septembre.

MONDAY, JULY 28, 1975

Dylan continues recording tracks at Columbia Studios in New York for what will yield next year's **Desire** album. Helping out at today's session on the song *Romance In Durango* is a Dobro-playing Eric Clapton.

Dylan arbeitet in den Columbia Studios in New York am seinem Album **Desire**, das im Folgejahr veröffent- licht wird. Bei dem Song *Romance In Durango* hilft Eric Clapton bei dieser Session an der Dobro aus.

Dylan continue à travailler dans les studios new- yorkais de Columbia, sur les titres qui constitueront l'album **Desire**. Ce jour-là, Dobro en bandoulière, Eric Clapton participe à l'enregistrement de la chanson *Romance In Durango*.

THURSDAY, OCTOBER 30, 1975

Dylan's initially low-key and spontaneous North American "Rolling Thunder Revue" tour starts at the Memorial Hall in Plymouth, Massachusetts. Tonight's opening show features Joan Baez, Roger McGuinn, Mick Ronson, Ramblin' Jack Elliott, Bobby Neuwirth, Ronee Blakley, and Allen Ginsberg, who all make their stage entrance wearing Lone Ranger masks.

Auftakt zur klein angelegten, spontanen Nordamerikatour „Rolling Thunder Revue" in der Memorial Hall in Plymouth, Massachusetts. Beim ersten Konzert treten neben Dylan Joan Baez, Roger McGuinn, Mick Ronson, Ramblin' Jack Elliott, Bobby Neuwirth, Ronee Blakley und Allen Ginsberg auf, die alle mit Lone-Ranger-Masken auf die Bühne kommen.

La nouvelle tournée nord-américaine « Rolling Thunder Revue » de Dylan, qu'il veut simple et spontanée, est lancée au Memorial Hall de Plymouth (Massachusetts). Pour ce premier concert, Joan Baez, Roger McGuinn, Mick Ronson, Ramblin' Jack Elliott, Bobby Neuwirth, Ronee Blakley et Allen Ginsberg montent successivement sur scène en arborant des masques de Lone Ranger.

MONDAY, DECEMBER 8, 1975

The "Rolling Thunder Revue" ends its first run at Madison Square Garden with "Night Of The Hurricane," a benefit for boxer and convicted murderer Rubin "Hurricane" Carter. Muhammad Ali acts as emcee and Roberta Flack guests. (Carter will be released from jail on bail, pending an appeal on March 21, 1976.)

Die „Rolling Thunder Revue" beendet ihre erste Saison im Madison Square Garden mit „Night Of The Hurricane", einem Benefizkonzert für den wegen Mordes verurteilten Boxer Rubin „Hurricane" Carter. Muhammad Ali ist Moderator und Roberta Flack Gaststar. (Carter wird am 21. März 1976 bis zum Berufungsverfahren gegen Kaution freigelassen.)

La première partie de la tournée « Rolling Thunder Revue » s'achève au Madison Square Garden avec « Night Of The Hurricane », un concert de charité organisé au profit du boxeur Rubin « Hurricane » Carter, accusé de meurtre. Mohammed Ali joue le Monsieur Loyal et Roberta Flack figure parmi les invités. (Carter sera libéré sous caution et jugé en appel à partir du 21 mars 1976.)

THURSDAY, NOVEMBER 25, 1976

After 16 years together, The Band make their farewell appearance on Thanksgiving Day at San Francisco's Winterland Ballroom—the scene of their first concert as The Band. A grand affair—organized by promoter Bill Graham and including a buffet, chandeliers, and an orchestra—it costs $25 a ticket and is dubbed "The Last Waltz." The four-hour concert sees the group joined by an endless roster of rock luminaries: Eric Clapton, Ringo Starr, Neil Diamond, Emmylou Harris, Joni Mitchell, Van Morrison, Muddy Waters, Neil Young, Dr. John, Ronnie Wood, Bobby Charles, Ronnie Hawkins, The Staple Singers, Paul Butterfield, and, of course, Dylan. The event is filmed for posterity by director Martin Scorsese. Backed by The Band, Dylan

sings *Baby Let Me Follow You Down, Hazel, I Don't Believe You (She Acts Like We Never Have Met), Forever Young,* and *I Shall Be Released,* on which he is joined by an all-star cast.

Nach 16 gemeinsamen Jahren gibt The Band am Thanksgiving Day ihr legendäres Abschiedskonzert im Winterland Ballroom in San Francisco – wo sie auch ihren ersten Auftritt als The Band hatte. Es ist ein opulentes, von Bill Graham veranstaltetes Fest mit Büffet, Kronleuchtern und Orchester – die Karten für „The Last Waltz" kosten 25 Dollar. Bei dem vierstündigen Konzert kommt ein endloses Defilee von Rockgrößen zu der Gruppe auf die Bühne: Eric Clapton, Ringo Starr, Neil Diamond, Emmylou Harris, Joni Mitchell,

Van Morrison, Muddy Waters, Neil Young, Dr. John, Ronnie Wood, Bobby Charles, Ronnie Hawkins, The Staple Singers, Paul Butterfield und natürlich Bob Dylan. Das Großereignis wird von Filmregisseur Martin Scorsese für die Nachwelt festgehalten. Begleitet von The Band singt Dylan *Baby Let Me Follow You Down*, *Hazel*, *I Don't Believe You (She Acts Like We Never Have Met)*, *Forever Young* und *I Shall Be Released*, das letzte Stück zusammen mit einem All-Star-Ensemble.

Après seize années ensemble, The Band fait ses adieux à la scène le jour de Thanksgiving, au Winterland Ballroom de San Francisco – où il avait joué pour la première fois. L'événement, surnommé « La Dernière Valse », est célébré en grande pompe par le pro-

moteur Bill Graham, avec buffet, chandeliers et orchestres – le ticket d'entrée coûte 25 dollars. Au cours des quatre heures de concert, le groupe est rejoint par une ribambelle de grands noms du rock : Eric Clapton, Ringo Starr, Neil Diamond, Emmylou Harris, Joni Mitchell, Van Morrison, Muddy Waters, Neil Young, Dr. John, Ronnie Wood, Bobby Charles, Ronnie Hawkins, The Staple Singers, Paul Butterfield et, bien sûr, Dylan. La soirée est filmée pour la postérité par le réalisateur Martin Scorsese. Dylan chante *Baby Let Me Follow You Down, Hazel, I Don't Believe You (She Acts Like We Never Have Met), Forever Young* et *I Shall Be Released*, dernier titre pour lequel il est accompagné par un magnifique plateau d'artistes.

WEDNESDAY, JANUARY 25, 1978

Dylan's four-hour-long movie, "Renaldo And Clara," opens in Los Angeles and New York. Written and directed by and starring Dylan, it also features his ex-wife Sara, Joan Baez, Ronnie Hawkins, Bob Neuwirth, Allen Ginsberg, Harry Dean Stanton, and Sam Shepard. Much of it was filmed during the 1975 "Rolling Thunder Revue."

Dylans vier Stunden langer Film „Renaldo And Clara" hat Premiere in Los Angeles und New York. Dylan schrieb das Drehbuch, führt Regie und spielt die Hauptrolle neben seiner Exfrau Sara, Joan Baez,

Ronnie Hawkins, Bob Neuwirth, Allen Ginsberg, Harry Dean Stanton und Sam Shepard. Ein Großteil des Films entstand 1975 bei der „Rolling Thunder Revue".

Première à Los Angeles et New York du film de quatre heures « Renaldo And Clara », écrit et réalisé par Dylan, qui joue le rôle principal. Dans le casting figurent aussi son ex-femme Sara, Joan Baez, Ronnie Hawkins, Bob Neuwirth, Allen Ginsberg, Harry Dean Stanton et Sam Shepard. Une grande partie a été filmée pendant la « Rolling Thunder Revue » de 1975.

"But people would not like the idea of Bob Dylan in a movie that was not a singing movie. They think I'm Gene Autry or Roy Rogers."
„Die Vorstellung von Bob Dylan in einem Film ohne Musik gefällt den Leuten nicht. Sie halten mich für Gene Autry oder Roy Rogers."
« Mais les gens n'aiment pas l'idée que Bob Dylan joue dans un film qui ne soit pas musical. Ils me prennent pour Gene Autry ou Roy Rogers. »
BOB DYLAN, LOS ANGELES TIMES, JANUARY 22, 1978

SATURDAY, JULY 15, 1978

"The Picnic At Blackbushe Aerodrome," with Dylan, Eric Clapton, Graham Parker, and Joan Armatrading, is staged at Blackbushe Airport, near Camberley in Surrey, before a crowd estimated at 200,000. Dylan—who took the train to get to the airfield venue—is joined by Clapton at the end of his three-hour set on *Forever Young.* 90,000 tickets for his concerts at Earls Court, London—his first British shows since the Isle of Wight Festival in 1969—sell out in eight hours.

„The Picnic At Blackbushe Aerodrome" mit Dylan, Eric Clapton, Graham Parker und Joan Armatrading ist ein Open-Air-Festival auf dem Blackbushe Airport in der Nähe von Camberley in England mit ca. 200.000 Zuschauern. Dylan – der mit dem Zug zum Veranstaltungsort gefahren ist – beendet sein Drei-Stunden-

Konzert zusammen mit Clapton mit dem Song *Forever Young.* Die neunzigtausend Karten für seine Konzerte im Earls Court, London – seine ersten Auftritte auf britischem Boden seit dem Isle of Wight Festival 1969 – sind innerhalb von acht Stunden ausverkauft.

Dylan, Eric Clapton, Graham Parker et Joan Armatrading sont à l'affiche du pique-nique de l'aérodrome de Blackbushe, près de Camberley, dans le Surrey, devant environ 200 000 personnes. Dylan est venu en train. Clapton le rejoint sur scène à la fin de son set de trois heures pour interpréter avec lui *Forever Young.* Quatre-vingt-dix mille tickets se sont vendus en huit heures pour ses concerts londoniens d'Earls Court – ses premières dates en Grande-Bretagne depuis le Festival de l'Île de Wight en 1969.

*"I like America, just as everybody else does.
I love America, I gotta say that. But America will be judged."*
*„Ich mag Amerika, wie alle anderen auch. Ich muss schon sagen,
ich liebe Amerika. Aber Amerika wird gerichtet werden."*
*« J'aime l'Amérique, comme tout le monde. J'adore l'Amérique,
il faut que je le dise. Mais l'Amérique sera jugée pour ses actes. »*
BOB DYLAN, ONSTAGE, GAMMAGE CENTER, TEMPE, ARIZONA

MONDAY, APRIL 30, 1979

Following a three-month Bible class at the Vineyard Christian Fellowship's School of Discipleship in Los Angeles, the born-again Dylan begins recording an album of original gospel songs in Muscle Shoals, Alabama, with guest musicians Mark Knopfler and Pick Withers of Dire Straits working alongside Muscle Shoals regulars Barry Beckett (who coproduces with Jerry Wexler) and Tim Drummond. The five-day session will result in 12 new tracks, which will make up his new album, ***Slow Train Coming***.

Nach einem dreimonatigen Bibelstudium in der Vineyard Christian Fellowship's School of Discipleship in Los Angeles beginnt der nun bekennende Christ Dylan mit den Aufnahmen zu einem Album mit Original-Gospelstücken in Muscle Shoals, Alabama. Gastmusiker sind Mark Knopfler und Pick Withers von den Dire Straits und die Muscle Shoals-Studiomusiker Barry Beckett (der zusammen mit Jerry Wexler auch produziert) und Tim Drummond. Bei der fünftägigen Session entstehen die zwölf neuen Titel des nächsten Albums ***Slow Train Coming***.

Dylan suit trois mois d'enseignement biblique à l'École des disciples du Vineyard Christian Fellowship de Los Angeles. Chrétien *born again* (« né de nouveau »), il commence l'enregistrement d'un album de chansons religieuses à Muscle Shoals (Alabama), avec la participation de Mark Knopfler et de Pick Withers, de Dire Straits, et des musiciens de Muscle Shoals, Barry Beckett (qui coproduit le disque avec Jerry Wexler) et Tim Drummond. De cette séance de cinq jours naîtront douze titres qui constitueront son nouvel album, ***Slow Train Coming***.

SATURDAY, OCTOBER 20, 1979

Dylan is the musical guest on NBC-TV's Eric Idle-hosted "Saturday Night Live," performing *Gotta Serve Somebody, I Believe In You,* and *When You Gonna Wake Up?*

Dylan ist zu Gast bei der NBC-Kultsendung „Saturday Night Live" mit Eric Idle als Moderator und spielt *Gotta Serve Somebody, I Believe In You* und *When You Gonna Wake Up?*

Dylan est l'invité musical de l'émission de NBC « Saturday Night Live », présentée par Eric Idle. Il interprète *Gotta Serve Somebody, I Believe In You* et *When You Gonna Wake Up?*

THE 1980^S

DIE 1980ER

LES ANNÉES 1980

"I didn't expect this. The first person I want to thank is the Lord."
„Damit habe ich nicht gerechnet. Am meisten muss ich mich dafür beim Herrn Jesus bedanken."
« Je ne m'y attendais pas. La première personne que je veux remercier, c'est le Seigneur. »
BOB DYLAN – ON RECEIVING HIS GRAMMY

WEDNESDAY, FEBRUARY 27, 1980

Having never been nominated in an illustrious 20-year recording career, Dylan wins Best Rock Vocal Performance, Male, for the gospel-tinged *Gotta Serve Somebody* at the 22nd annual Grammy Awards.

Dylan, der in den 20 Jahren seiner glänzenden Plattenkarriere nie für einen Grammy nominiert worden ist, gewinnt den Preis für den Gospelsong *Gotta Serve Somebody* bei der 22. Grammy-Verleihung in der Kategorie „Beste männliche Gesangsdarbietung – Rock".

Jamais présélectionné en vingt ans de carrière musicale, Dylan remporte le prix de la Meilleure performance vocale masculine dans la catégorie Rock pour son titre d'influence gospel *Gotta Serve Somebody* au cours de la 22ᵉ cérémonie des Grammy Awards.

SUNDAY, NOVEMBER 9, 1980

The first of 12 shows at the Warfield Theatre in San Francisco. The guest musicians through the two weeks include Carlos Santana, Mike Bloomfield, Jerry Garcia, and Roger McGuinn.

Der erste von zwölf Auftritten im Warfield Theatre in San Francisco. Zu den Gastmusikern zählen Carlos Santana, Mike Bloomfield, Jerry Garcia und Roger McGuinn.

Première de ses douze dates au Warfield Theatre de San Francisco. Plusieurs invités de marque se succèdent aux côtés de Dylan, parmi lesquels Carlos Santana, Mike Bloomfield, Jerry Garcia et Roger McGuinn.

MONDAY, JANUARY 12, 1981

The Recording Industry Association of America donates some 800 rock albums—among them Dylan's now seminal double LP *Blonde On Blonde*—to the Library of Congress.

Die Recording Industry Association of America stiftet der Library of Congress ca. 800 Rock-LPs – darunter auch Dylans bereits als Meilenstein geltendes Doppelalbum *Blonde On Blonde*.

La Recording Industry Association of America (association des professionnels américains du disque) fait don à la bibliothèque du Congrès de 800 albums de rock, parmi lesquels le double-album légendaire de Dylan *Blonde On Blonde*.

THURSDAY, MARCH 26, 1981

The first sessions for what will be the **Shot Of Love** album take place at Rundown Studios in Santa Monica. Either side of its August release, Dylan will play a total of 54 dates in Europe and North America promoting the record.

Die ersten Aufnahmen für das Album **Shot Of Love**, das im August veröffentlicht werden soll, finden in den Rundown Studios in Santa Monica statt. Um die neue Platte zu promoten, tritt Dylan bei insgesamt 54 Konzerten in Europa und Nordamerika auf.

Premières sessions d'enregistrement de l'album **Shot Of Love** aux studios Rundown de Santa Monica. Dylan donnera au total 54 concerts de promotion en Europe et en Amérique du Nord.

MONDAY, MARCH 15, 1982

Dylan is inducted into the Songwriters Hall of Fame at the 13th annual dinner held at New York's Hilton Hotel.

Dylan wird bei der 13. alljährlichen Gala im New Yorker Hilton Hotel in die Songwriters Hall of Fame aufgenommen.

Dylan entre au Hall of Fame des auteurs-compositeurs de chansons lors du 13ᵉ gala annuel donné à l'hôtel Hilton de New York.

"I think this is pretty amazing because I can't read or write a note of music. Thank you."
„Ich finde das ziemlich unglaublich, da ich keine einzige Note lesen order schreiben kann. Danke."
« Je trouve ça plutôt incroyable dans la mesure où je ne sais ni écrire ni lire la musique. Merci. »
BOB DYLAN

SUNDAY, JUNE 6, 1982

Dylan joins Stevie Wonder, Jackson Browne, Crosby, Stills and Nash, Linda Ronstadt, Dan Fogelberg, Tom Petty, and Joan Baez (with whom he duets on *Blowin' In The Wind* and *With God On Our Side*) in the "Peace Sunday: 'We Have A Dream'" antinuclear concert, to launch Peace Week, at the Rose Bowl in Pasadena, California, before a crowd of 85,000.

Dylan tritt beim Anti-Atomwaffen-Konzert „Peace Sunday: ‚We Have A Dream'" zusammen mit Stevie Wonder, Jackson Browne, Crosby, Stills and Nash, Linda Ronstadt, Dan Fogelberg, Tom Petty und Joan Baez (mit der er zusammen *Blowin' In The Wind* und *With God On Our Side* singt) vor 85.000 Leuten auf, als Auftakt zur Peace Week in der Rose Bowl in Pasadena, Kalifornien.

Dylan retrouve Stevie Wonder, Jackson Browne, Crosby, Stills and Nash, Linda Ronstadt, Dan Fogelberg, Tom Petty et Joan Baez (avec laquelle il chante *Blowin' In The Wind* et *With God On Our Side*) pour le concert antinucléaire « Peace Sunday: 'We Have A Dream' », qui inaugure la Semaine de la paix, au Rose Bowl de Pasadena (Californie), devant 85 000 personnes.

MONDAY, APRIL 11 TO TUESDAY, MAY 17, 1983

Dylan records the material for *Infidels*, produced with Mark Knopfler, at Studio A in the Power Station, New York. The album will be released in November.

Dylan nimmt das Material für die zusammen mit Mark Knopfler produzierte LP *Infidels* im Studio A in der Power Station, New York, auf. Das Album wird im November veröffentlicht.

Dylan enregistre les titres d'*Infidels*, qu'il produit avec Mark Knopfler, au Studio A de Power Station, à New York. L'album sort en novembre.

THURSDAY, MARCH 22, 1984

In an unlikely pairing of guests, Dylan and Liberace both appear on NBC-TV's "Late Night With David Letterman." Dylan plays three songs backed by young rock band The Plugz.

Dylan und Liberace sind die denkbar gegensätzlichen Gaststars der Talkshow „Late Night With David Letterman". Dylan spielt zusammen mit der jungen Rockband The Plugz drei Stücke.

Couple improbable, Dylan et Liberace sont invités ensemble à l'émission « Late Night With David Letterman », sur la chaîne NBC. Dylan joue trois titres avec le jeune groupe de rock The Plugz.

SUNDAY, JULY 8, 1984

Dylan's latest European tour, headlining a bill that features Santana, UB40, and In Tua Nua, comes to an end at Slane Castle in Ireland. Following yesterday's gig at Wembley Stadium in London, which saw Dylan joined onstage by Eric Clapton, Van Morrison, Chrissie Hynde, and Carlos Santana, Morrison again wanders onstage, joining in on *It's All Over Now, Baby Blue* and on his own classic, *Tupelo Honey*. U2's Bono, sent to interview Dylan before the show for the Irish rock magazine **Hot Press**, winds up duetting with him on *Blowin' In The Wind* and *Leopard-Skin Pill-Box Hat*.

Dylans Europatournee mit Santana, UB40 und In Tua Nua endet an diesem Tag am Slane Castle in Irland. Am Vortag im Wembley Stadium in London kamen Eric Clapton, Van Morrison, Chrissie Hynde und Carlos Santana zu Dylan auf die Bühne. In Irland erscheint Morrison wieder auf der Bühne und singt mit bei *It's All Over Now, Baby Blue* und seinem Klassiker *Tupelo Honey*. Bono von U2, der Dylan vor dem Konzert für das irische Rockmagazin **Hot Press** interviewt hat, singt dann überraschend *Blowin' In The Wind* und *Leopard-Skin Pill-Box Hat* mit ihm.

La nouvelle tournée européenne de Dylan, avec notamment Santana, UB40 ou In Tua Nua en première partie, s'achève à Slane Castle, en Irlande. La veille, au stade de Wembley, à Londres, Eric Clapton, Van Morrison, Chrissie Hynde et Carlos Santana ont participé au concert. Morrison revient sur scène pour chanter avec Dylan *It's All Over Now, Baby Blue*, puis son propre titre *Tupelo Honey*. Le chanteur de U2, Bono, qui a interviewé Dylan avant le spectacle pour le magazine de rock irlandais **Hot Press**, chante avec lui *Blowin' In The Wind* et *Leopard-Skin Pill-Box Hat*.

MONDAY, JANUARY 28, 1985

In the midst of recording material for his upcoming *Empire Burlesque*, Dylan joins 45 other top recording artists at the A&M Studios in Hollywood, following this year's American Music Awards celebrations in Los Angeles. Greeted by a warning notice from producer Quincy Jones to "check your egos at the door," all arrive in separate limousines, except Bruce Springsteen, who is in a truck. They are there at the behest of Jones, Harry Belafonte (who has been inspired by the efforts of Bob Geldof's Band Aid single), and Ken Kragen (Kenny Rogers' manager). The song to be recorded, *We Are The World*, has been written by Michael Jackson and Lionel Richie in just two hours, following three days of preparation. Inside the studio, a strip of named tape for each performer has been stuck on the floor, forming a semicircular ensemble. Those chosen for lead vocals will later be grouped close to one of six microphones, as their efforts will be recorded after the choruses have been taped. The end result features 21 solo vocal segments, of which Dylan's is the 20th. After 10 hours, only Richie and Jones remain, putting the final touches on an extraordinary recording that will be released under the fundraising banner USA for Africa.

Dylan unterbricht die Aufnahmen zu seinem nächsten Album *Empire Burlesque* und gesellt sich nach den Feierlichkeiten der American Music Awards in Los Angeles zu 45 anderen berühmten Musikern in den A&M Studios in Hollywood. Von Produzent Quincy Jones vorgewarnt, alle müssten „ihre Egos an der Garderobe abgeben", treffen sie in einzelnen Limousinen vor Ort ein, außer Bruce Springsteen, der im Truck anreist. Sie kommen auf Bitten von Quincy Jones, Harry Belafonte (der sich von Bob Geldofs Band Aid-Single inspiriert fühlte) und Ken Kragen (Manager von Kenny Rogers). Aufgenommen werden soll das Lied *We Are The World*, nach dreitägiger Vorbereitung in nur zwei Stunden von Michael Jackson und Lionel Richie geschrieben. Im Aufnahmestudio wurde für jeden Mitwirkenden ein Klebeband mit dem Namen auf dem Boden angebracht, sodass das Ensemble im Halbkreis zusammensteht. Später gruppieren sich die für die Soloparts ausgewählten Sänger um sechs Mikrofone, ihr Beitrag wird aufgenommen, nachdem die Refrains im Kasten sind. Die Endfassung enthält 21 Solovokalabschnitte, Dylans ist der zwanzigste. Nach zehn Stunden sind nur noch Richie und Jones da und legen letzte Hand an diese einmalige Aufnahme, die unter dem Motto „USA for Africa" einem guten Zweck zukommen wird.

Alors qu'il travaille sur les titres de son prochain album, *Empire Burlesque*, Dylan rejoint 45 autres chanteurs aux studios A&M de Hollywood, juste après la cérémonie des American Music Awards. Accueillis par un avertissement ferme du producteur Quincy Jones, qui leur demande de «laisser leur ego au vestiaire», ils arrivent à bord de limousines séparées, à part Bruce Springsteen, qui conduit une camionnette. Ils ont été conviés par Jones, Harry Belafonte (inspiré par le Band Aid de Bob Geldof) et Ken Kragen (l'agent de Kenny Rogers). La chanson qu'ils viennent enregistrer ensemble, *We Are The World*, a été écrite par Michael Jackson et Lionel Richie en à peine deux heures, après trois jours de préparation. Dans le studio, des bandes de scotch sur lesquelles sont inscrits les noms des artistes ont été collées au sol en arcs de cercle. Ceux qui ont été choisis comme voix lead sont regroupés autour d'un des six micros et chantent leurs parties une fois les chœurs enregistrés. Vingt-et-un segments vocaux en solo sont ainsi obtenus ; Dylan chante le vingtième. Après dix heures de travail, il ne reste plus dans le studio que Richie et Jones, qui mettent la dernière main à ce morceau extraordinaire, dont les bénéfices seront reversés à USA for Africa.

"You know while I'm here, I just hope that some of the money that's raised for the people in Africa, maybe they could just take just a little bit of it, one or two million maybe, and use it to, maybe use it to pay the mortgages on some of the farms, that the farmers here owe to the banks."

„Ich hoffe, dass ein bisschen von dem Geld, das hier für die Leute in Afrika zusammengebracht wird, dass ein kleines bisschen davon, ein oder zwei Millionen vielleicht, genommen wird, um damit die Hypotheken zu bezahlen, mit denen die Farmer hier bei den Banken verschuldet sind."

« Vous savez, j'aimerais bien qu'une partie de l'argent collecté pour la population en Afrique, peut-être qu'ils pourraient juste en prendre une petite partie, disons un ou deux millions, et l'utiliser pour, peut-être pour racheter les hypothèques de ces fermiers d'ici qui ne peuvent plus rembourser les banques. »

BOB DYLAN

SATURDAY, JULY 13, 1985

Dylan closes the historic fundraiser "Live Aid" at the JFK Stadium in Philadelphia, Pennsylvania, backed by the Rolling Stones' Keith Richards and Ronnie Wood on guitars. In a broadcast that switches between joint venues—Wembley Stadium in London, in the presence of the Prince and Princess of Wales, and the JFK Stadium—the world's biggest rock acts participate in a global fundraising event. Watched by a television audience estimated at 2 billion people, with telethons in 22 countries, "Live Aid" raises some $70 million, becoming a defining cooperative moment in the rock era.

Mit seinem Auftritt setzt Dylan den Schlusspunkt beim legendären Benefizkonzerts „Live Aid" im JFK Stadium in Philadelphia, Pennsylvania; Keith Richards und Ronnie Wood von den Rolling Stones begleiten ihn an der Gitarre. Bei der Live-Übertragung wird zwischen den beiden Veranstaltungsorten - zwischen dem Wembley Stadium in London in Anwesenheit von Prinz Charles und Prinzessin Diana und dem JFK Stadium - hin- und hergeschaltet. Die berühmtesten Rockstars der Welt nehmen an diesem weltweiten Mammutevent teil. „Live Aid" wird von geschätzten 2 Milliarden Fernsehzuschauern in 22 Ländern verfolgt, bringt ca. 70 Mio. Dollar ein und wird zur größten Kooperative in der Geschichte der Rockmusik.

Dylan clôt le célèbre concert de charité « Live Aid » au JFK Stadium de Philadelphie, accompagné par Keith Richards et Ronnie Wood, des Rolling Stones, à la guitare. Cette vaste entreprise de collecte de fonds a lieu simultanément au Stade de Wembley, à Londres, en présence du prince Charles et de Lady Diana, et les deux concerts sont diffusés en alternance par les télévisions du monde entier. La retransmission est suivie par quelque deux milliards de téléspectateurs, qui peuvent faire des promesses de dons par téléphone dans 22 pays. Le « Live Aid » permet de collecter 70 millions de dollars et montre une scène rock concernée par les problèmes du monde.

SUNDAY, SEPTEMBER 22, 1985

Backed by Tom Petty & The Heartbreakers, Dylan performs at the inaugural "Farm Aid" benefit, at the University of Illinois, Champaign, Illinois. Inspired by his comment at "Live Aid," "Farm Aid" is held amid massive Unites States media interest at an all-day festival at the University of Illinois' Memorial Stadium in Champaign, Illinois, before a crowd of 79,000 fans, raising $1,450,000, plus a further estimated $6 million in donations. Willie Nelson, who joins Dylan for three of his numbers, John Mellencamp, Neil Young, B. B. King, Roy Orbison, the queen of country Loretta Lynn, Billy Joel, and Randy Newman—who perform Sail Away, Political Science, Only The Good Die Young, and Stagger Lee together—are among 60 artists taking part. The event— chiefly organized by Nelson, Mellencamp, and Young— will become an annual music festival into the '90s.

Mit Unterstützung von Tom Petty & The Heartbreakers spielt Dylan beim ersten „Farm Aid"-Benefizkonzert an der University of Illinois, Champaign, Illinois. „Farm Aid" entstand als Antwort auf Dylans Kommentar bei „Live Aid" und wird unter massivem Aufgebot der US-Medien und einem ganztägigen Festival im Memorial Stadium der University of Illinois in Champaign, Illinois, vor 79.000 Fans durchgeführt. Es kommen 1.450.000 Dollar sowie geschätzte weitere 6 Mio. Dollar an Spenden zusammen. Zu den ca.

60 Künstlern, die teilnehmen, gehören Willie Nelson, der bei drei von Dylans Stücken mitsingt, John Mellencamp, Neil Young, B. B. King, Roy Orbison, die „Queen of Country" Loretta Lynn, Billy Joel und Randy Newman, die gemeinsam Sail Away, Political Science, Only The Good Die Young und Stagger Lee singen. Das zum großen Teil von Nelson, Mellencamp und Young organisierte Event entwickelt sich in den 1990ern zu einem alljährlich stattfindenden Musikfestival.

Accompagné par Tom Petty & The Heartbreakers, Dylan participe au premier concert «Farm Aid» organisé par l'université de l'Illinois dans son Memorial Stadium, à Champaign. Inspiré par sa petite phrase du «Live Aid», la journée de collecte de fonds est largement couverte par les médias américains et rapporte 1 450 000 dollars; six autres millions sont directement collectés auprès des 79 000 personnes venues écouter les soixante artistes présents, parmi lesquels Willie Nelson, qui se joint à Dylan pour trois chansons, John Mellencamp, Neil Young, B. B. King, Roy Orbison, la reine de la musique country Loretta Lynn, Billy Joel et Randy Newman – qui chantent ensemble Sail Away, Political Science, Only The Good Die Young et Stagger Lee. L'événement, organisé de main de maître par Nelson, Mellencamp et Young, deviendra un festival annuel dans les années 1990.

MONDAY, JANUARY 20, 1986

The first Martin Luther King Jr. Day is celebrated with concerts in Atlanta, New York City, and Washington, D. C., where Dylan performs *I Shall Be Released* and *Blowin' In The Wind* backed by Peter, Paul, and Mary and Stevie Wonder, and duets with Wonder on *The Bells Of Freedom*.

Der gerade zum Feiertag erhobene erste Martin Luther King Day wird mit Konzerten in Atlanta, New York City und Washington, D. C. gefeiert, wo Dylan zusammen mit Peter, Paul, and Mary und Stevie Wonder *I Shall Be Released* und *Blowin' In The Wind* singt und zusammen mit Wonder *The Bells Of Freedom*.

La première Journée Martin Luther King est célébrée par des concerts à Atlanta, New York et Washington, où Dylan joue *I Shall Be Released* et *Blowin' In The Wind*, accompagné par Peter, Paul, and Mary et Stevie Wonder; il chante aussi *The Bells Of Freedom* en duo avec Wonder.

MONDAY, JUNE 9, 1986

Following an appearance at Friday's "A Conspiracy of Hope" benefit for Amnesty International at the Forum in Inglewood, California, Dylan embarks on the North American leg of his "True Confessions" tour, on which the singer is backed by Tom Petty & The Heartbreakers, at the Sports Arena in San Diego. The 41-date tour, Dylan's first in the United States for five years, will see him joined by a host of guests as he traverses the country, including Bob Seger in Clarkston,

Michigan, Ronnie Wood in New York, Al Kooper in East Rutherford, New Jersey, Annie Lennox and Dave Stewart in Inglewood, and The Grateful Dead, who show up more than once.

Nachdem Dylan drei Tage zuvor beim Benefizkonzert „A Conspiracy of Hope" für Amnesty International im Forum in Inglewood, Kalifornien, aufgetreten ist, startet er seine „True Confessions" Tour in der Sports Arena in San Diego und wird von Tom Petty & The Heartbreakers begleitet. Es ist Dylans erste USA-Tournee seit fünf Jahren. Ein Geschwader von Gästen kommt auf seiner Reise durch das Land mit 41 Stationen zu ihm auf die Bühne: Bob Seger in Clarkston, Michigan, Ronnie Wood in New York, Al Kooper in East Rutherford, New Jersey, Annie Lennox und Dave Stewart in Inglewood, und die Grateful Dead sind bei mehreren Terminen mit von der Partie.

Après une apparition au concert d'Amnesty International « A Conspiracy of Hope » au Forum d'Inglewood (Californie) le vendredi précédent, Dylan démarre la partie américaine de sa tournée « True Confessions », sur laquelle il est accompagné par Tom Petty & The Heartbreakers, à la Sports Arena de San Diego. Au fil des 41 dates de la tournée, la première de Dylan aux États-Unis depuis cinq ans, il accueillera sur scène de nombreux artistes : Bob Seger à Clarkston (Michigan), Ronnie Wood à New York, Al Kooper à East Rutherford (New Jersey), Annie Lennox et Dave Stewart à Inglewood, et les Grateful Dead à plusieurs reprises.

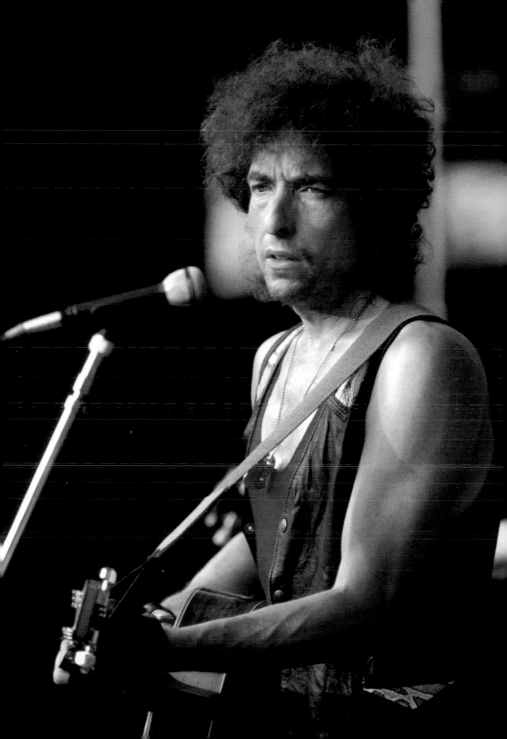

136

SATURDAY, JULY 4 - 26, 1987

Dylan and The Grateful Dead, who back his set as well as playing their own (inevitably) longer one, perform six United States dates.

Dylan und die Grateful Dead treten bei sechs Konzerten in den USA zusammen auf. In der einen Hälfte des Konzerts erscheinen die Grateful Dead als

Dylans Backing Band, in der anderen (natürlich) wesentlich längeren Hälfte spielen sie ihre eigenen Stücke.

Dylan et les Grateful Dead partagent l'affiche de six concerts américains; le groupe l'accompagne, mais joue surtout ses propres morceaux.

138

WEDNESDAY, JANUARY 20, 1988
  With many of the founders of rock 'n' roll already
members of the Rock and Roll Hall of Fame, their pro-
genitors—The Beatles, The Beach Boys, and Bob
Dylan—are among those inducted at the third annual
dinner at the Waldorf-Astoria Hotel in New York.

Bruce Springsteen inducts Dylan. Appropriately, one
of the Early Performers inducted is Woody Guthrie.
  Viele der Gründerväter des Rock 'n' Roll sind
bereits Mitglieder der Rock and Roll Hall of Fame;
einige ihrer wichtigsten Nachkommen – The Beatles,
The Beach Boys und Bob Dylan – werden beim dritten

Jahresdinner im Waldorf-Astoria Hotel in New York neu aufgenommen. Bruce Springsteen führt Dylan ein. Passenderweise wird auch Woody Guthrie als einer der frühen Vertreter aufgenommen.

Alors que la plupart des figures fondatrices du rock font déjà partie du Rock and Roll Hall of Fame, leurs «poulains» – les Beatles, les Beach Boys et Bob Dylan – sont intronisés lors du 3ᵉ gala annuel organisé à l'hôtel Waldorf-Astoria de New York. Bruce Springsteen parraine Dylan. Comme il se doit, Woody Guthrie fait partie des auteurs-compositeurs de la première heure honorés par l'académie.

"A remarkable sophisticated musical culture developed, considering there were no managers or agents ... they found themselves the object of interest among many less-developed species—nightclub owners, tour operators, and recording executives."

„Eine hoch entwickelte Musikkultur entstand, die umso bemerkenswerter war, da es weder Manager noch Agenten gab ... Sie wurden zum Objekt der Begierde einer weniger hoch entwickelten Spezies: Besitzer von Musikclubs, Tourneeveranstalter und Manager von Plattenfirmen."

« Une culture musicale remarquablement sophistiquée prit son essor, remarquable parce qu'elle n'avait ni managers ni agents... Ils devinrent l'objet d'un grand intérêt parmi les spécimens de nombreuses autres espèces moins développées – propriétaires de boîtes de nuit, voyagistes et patrons de maisons de disques. »

TRAVELING WILBURYS LINER NOTES

SUNDAY, APRIL 3, 1988

The Traveling Wilburys quintet, a one-off group comprising Lucky Wilbury (Dylan), Otis Wilbury (Jeff Lynne), Nelson Wilbury (George Harrison), Charlie T. Jr. (Tom Petty), and Lefty Wilbury (Roy Orbison), begin recording *Handle With Care* at Lucky's garage studio in Malibu, California. They will finish recording sessions for a complete album at Eurythmic Dave Stewart's home studio in Los Angeles during May. Produced by Otis and Nelson, *Traveling Wilburys* will be released by the Wilbury Record Company on October 18, set for glowing reviews and triple-platinum United States sales.

Das Quintett The Traveling Wilburys, eine Ad-hoc-Band, bestehend aus Lucky Wilbury (Dylan), Otis Wilbury (Jeff Lynne), Nelson Wilbury (George Harrison), Charlie T. Jr. (Tom Petty) und Lefty Wilbury (Roy Orbison), beginnt mit den Aufnahmen zu *Handle With Care* in Luckys Garagenstudio in Malibu, Kalifornien. Im Mai stellen sie das Album im heimischen Tonstudio von Dave Stewart (Eurythmics) in Los Angeles fertig. Das von Otis und Nelson produzierte Album *Traveling Wilburys* wird am 18. Oktober von der Wilbury Record Company veröffentlicht und erzielt hervorragende Kritiken und dreifaches Platin in den USA.

Les Traveling Wilburys, un quintette éphémère composé de Lucky Wilbury (Dylan), Otis Wilbury (Jeff Lynne), Nelson Wilbury (George Harrison), Charlie T. Jr. (Tom Petty) et Lefty Wilbury (Roy Orbison), commencent l'enregistrement de *Handle With Care* dans le garage de Lucky aménagé en studio, à Malibu (Californie). Ils le terminent en mai dans le studio personnel de Dave Stewart, d'Eurythmics, à Los Angeles. La Wilbury Record Company sort *Traveling Wilburys*, produit par Otis et Nelson, le 18 octobre. Encensé par la critique, il deviendra triple album de platine aux États-Unis.

SUNDAY, SEPTEMBER 24, 1989

"L'Chaim: To Life!" telethon on Chabad TV, with his son-in-law Peter Himmelman (married to his daughter Maria) and actor Harry Dean Stanton on guitars. They perform—as Chopped Liver—three songs, including *Hava Nagila*, with Dylan—whose new album, *Oh Mercy*, was released earlier in the week—contributing on flute and recorder.

„L'Chaim: To Life!"-Spendenmarathon auf Chabad TV. Dylan tritt mit seinem Schwiegersohn Peter Himmelman (verheiratet mit seiner Tochter Maria) und Schauspieler Harry Dean Stanton an der Gitarre auf. Unter dem Namen Chopped Liver bringen sie drei Songs, einer davon ist *Hava Nagila*. Dylan – dessen neues Album *Oh Mercy* Anfang der Woche herausgekommen ist - spielt Flöte.

Il participe au téléthon « L'Chaim: To Life! », sur Chabad TV, avec son gendre Peter Himmelman (marié à sa fille Maria) et l'acteur Harry Dean Stanton à la guitare. Ils jouent trois chansons – sous le nom de Chopped Liver - dont *Hava Nagila*. Dylan, dont le nouvel album *Oh Mercy*, est sorti à début de cette semaine, joue de la flûte et enregistre le set.

THE 1990ˢ

DIE 1990ER

LES ANNÉES 1990

TUESDAY, JANUARY 30, 1990

In Paris during a four-day stint at the Rex Theater, Bob Dylan is awarded France's highest cultural honor, the Commandeur dans l'Ordre des Arts et des Lettres, by Minister Jack Lang in a ceremony at the Palais Royal.

Während eines viertägigen Gastspiels im Grand Rex in Paris wird Bob Dylan die höchste kulturelle Auszeichnung Frankreichs zuteil: Minister Jack Lang ernennt ihn während einer Feierstunde im Palais Royal zum Commandeur dans l'Ordre des Arts et des Lettres.

À Paris pour une série de quatre dates au Grand Rex, Bob Dylan est honoré de la plus grande distinction culturelle française, la médaille de Commandeur dans l'Ordre des Arts et des Lettres, par le ministre de la Culture Jack Lang.

SATURDAY, FEBRUARY 24, 1990

Dylan, three of the Byrds, Bonnie Raitt, John Fogerty, Johnny Cash, Bruce Hornsby, B. B. King, k. d. lang, Was (Not Was), Dwight Yoakam, and others take part in the "Roy Orbison Concert Tribute To Benefit The Homeless." Most of the performers sing Orbison numbers, except Dylan, who joins Roger McGuinn, David Crosby, and Chris Hillman on *He Was A Friend Of Mine* and *Mr. Tambourine Man*.

Dylan, drei Mitglieder der Byrds, Bonnie Raitt, John Fogerty, Johnny Cash, Bruce Hornsby, B. B. King, k. d. lang, Was (Not Was), Dwight Yoakam und andere nehmen am „Roy Orbison Concert Tribute To Benefit The Homeless". Die meisten spielen Orbison-Stücke, außer Dylan, der zusammen mit Roger McGuinn, David Crosby und Chris Hillman *He Was A Friend Of Mine* und *Mr. Tambourine Man* singt.

Dylan, trois membres des Byrds, Bonnie Raitt, John Fogerty, Johnny Cash, Bruce Hornsby, B. B. King, k. d. lang, Was (Not Was), Dwight Yoakam et d'autres participent au « Roy Orbison Concert Tribute To Benefit The Homeless ». La plupart des participants chantent des titres d'Orbison, sauf Dylan, qui joue *He Was A Friend of Mine* et *Mr. Tambourine Man* en compagnie de Roger McGuinn, David Crosby et Chris Hillman.

APRIL 1990
Sessions take place at Wilbury Mountain Studio in Bel Air, Los Angeles, for a second Traveling Wilburys album, cryptically titled *Traveling Wilburys Vol. 3*.

Sessions für das zweite Album der Traveling Wilburys mit dem rätselhaften Titel *Traveling Wilburys Vol. 3* im Wilbury Mountain Studio in Bel Air, Los Angeles.

Enregistrement au Wilbury Mountain Studio de Bel Air
(Los Angeles), du deuxième album des Traveling Wilburys, bizarrement intitulé *Traveling Wilburys Vol. 3*.

"I've been here for four years, and this is the best time I've ever had ...
We're not politically agreeing with Bob Dylan. We're just shifting all that
stuff aside and enjoying his music."
„Ich bin jetzt seit vier Jahren hier, und so viel Spaß haben wir hier noch
nie gehabt ... Politisch sind wir mit Bob Dylan nicht auf einer Linie. Aber
wir lassen das mal alles beiseite und freuen uns einfach an seiner Musik."
« Je suis ici depuis quatre ans, et c'est le meilleur moment que j'ai
passé... Nous ne partageons pas les opinions politiques de Bob Dylan.
Nous mettons tout ça de côté pour simplement apprécier sa musique. »
CADET STEVEN J. CAVIOLI JR.

SATURDAY, OCTOBER 13, 1990
Bob Dylan performs for 4,020 cadets in the Dwight
D. Eisenhower Hall at the United States Military Acad-
emy in West Point, New York, with hundreds of cadets
joining him on *Blowin' In The Wind*.
Bob Dylan spielt vor 4.020 Kadetten in der Dwight
D. Eisenhower Hall in der U.S. Military Academy in
West Point, New York. Bei *Blowin' In The Wind* singen
mehrere Hundert Jungsoldaten mit.
Bob Dylan joue pour 4 020 cadets réunis dans la
salle Dwight D. Eisenhower de l'académie militaire
américaine de West Point (New York) ; ils sont des cen-
taines à entonner avec lui les couplets de *Blowin' In
The Wind*.

"Well, my daddy he didn't leave me too much. You know he was a very simple man and he didn't leave me a lot but what he told me was this ... what he did say was ... son ... he said uh .... he said so many things you know ..... he said you know it's possible to become so defiled in this world that your own mother and father will abandon you, and if that happens God will always believe in your own ability to mend your own ways. Thank you."

„Sehr viel hat mir mein Daddy ja nicht hinterlassen. Er war ein sehr einfacher Mann und viel hat er mir nicht hinterlassen, aber eins hat er mir klargemacht ... also er sagte ... Sohn ... er sagte ... er hat mir eine Menge gesagt ... jedenfalls meinte er: Man kann in dieser Welt so tief sinken, dass deine eigenen Eltern dich aufgeben. Aber selbst wenn das passiert, wird Gott doch immer noch daran glauben, dass du dich bessern kannst. Danke schön."

« Eh bien, mon papa, il ne m'a pas laissé grand-chose. Vous savez, c'était un homme très simple et il avait peu de choses à me laisser, mais voici ce qu'il m'a dit... fiston... il a dit... euh... Il m'a dit tellement de choses, vous savez... Il a dit, tu vois, ce monde peut tellement te salir que ton propre père et ta propre mère t'abandonneront, et si cela arrive, Dieu croira toujours en ta capacité à t'amender. Merci. »

BOB DYLAN

WEDNESDAY, FEBRUARY 20, 1991

Dylan is presented with the National Academy of Recording Arts and Sciences Lifetime Achievement Award at the 33rd annual Grammy Awards ceremony, from Radio City Music Hall, New York, by Jack Nicholson. The special merit award is presented by vote of the Recording Academy's National Trustees to performers who, during their lifetimes, have made creative contributions of outstanding artistic significance to the field of recording.

Bei der 33. Grammy-Verleihung wird Dylans Lebenswerk mit dem National Academy of Recording Arts und Sciences Lifetime Achievement Award geehrt, der Preis wird ihm in der Radio City Music Hall in New York von Jack Nicholson überreicht. Diese begehrte Auszeichnung wird von der Recording Academy an Persönlichkeiten verliehen, die in ihrem Leben herausragende künstlerische Beiträge im Bereich der Schallplattenaufnahmen geleistet haben.

Dylan reçoit le prix de la National Academy of Recording Arts and Sciences pour l'ensemble de sa carrière lors de la 33ᵉ cérémonie annuelle des Grammy Awards, présentée depuis le Radio City Music Hall de New York par Jack Nicholson. Ce prix spécial est remis, après un vote des administrateurs de l'académie, à des artistes dont les créations ont contribué de façon importante à l'histoire de la musique.

FRIDAY, OCTOBER 16, 1992

The "Bob Dylan 30th Anniversary Concert Celebration" is held at New York's Madison Square Garden. Performers taking part include Eric Clapton, George Harrison, Roger McGuinn, Tom Petty, John Mellencamp, Booker T. & the MG's, Willie Nelson, Kris Kristofferson and Sinéad O'Connor. Dylan performs *Song To Woody, It's Alright Ma (I'm Only Bleeding)*, and *My Back Pages*, backed by Clapton, Harrison, McGuinn, and Petty, and the entire ensemble close the show with *Knockin' On Heaven's Door.*

Im Madison Square Garden New York wird die „Bob Dylan 30th Anniversary Concert Celebration" begangen. An diesem Abend spielen außerdem Eric Clapton, George Harrison, Roger McGuinn, Tom Petty, John Mellencamp, Booker T. & the MG's, Willie Nel-son, Kris Kristofferson und Sinéad O'Connor. Dylan selbst singt die Titel *Song To Woody, It's Alright Ma (I'm Only Bleeding)* und *My Back Pages*, unterstützt von Clapton, Harrison, McGuinn und Petty. Das gesamte Ensemble beschließt die Show mit *Knockin' On Heaven's Door.*

Concert pour les 30 ans de carrière de Bob Dylan au Madison Square Garden de New York. À l'affiche : Eric Clapton, George Harrison, Roger McGuinn, Tom Petty, John Mellencamp, Booker T. & the MG's, Willie Nelson, Kris Kristofferson et Sinéad O'Connor. Dylan joue *Song To Woody, It's Alright Ma (I'm Only Bleeding)* et *My Back Pages* avec Clapton, Harrison, McGuinn et Petty, et l'ensemble des musiciens présents chantent *Knockin' On Heaven's Door.*

SUNDAY, JANUARY 17, 1993

"A Call for Reunion: A Musical Celebration" during the presidential inaugural festivities for President Bill Clinton at the Lincoln Memorial. Dylan sings *Chimes Of Freedom* and also joins The Band and Stephen Stills for *I Shall Be Released* at the "Absolutely Unofficial Bluejeans Bash" at the National Building Museum in the evening.

Bei der Amtseinführung des neuen amerikanischen Präsidenten Bill Clinton am Lincoln Memorial gibt es auch ein Musikprogramm: „A Call for Reunion: A Musical Celebration". Dylan singt *Chimes Of Freedom* und

beim „Absolutely Unofficial Bluejeans Bash" am selben Abend im National Building Museum zusammen mit The Band und Stephen Stills *I Shall Be Released.*

« A Call for Reunion: A Musical Celebration », concert donné à l'occasion des célébrations d'investiture du président Bill Clinton au Lincoln Memorial. Dylan chante *Chimes Of Freedom* puis, dans la soirée, *I Shall Be Released* avec The Band et Stephen Stills, dans le cadre de l'« Absolutely Unofficial Bluejeans Bash » qui se tient au National Building Museum.

SUNDAY, AUGUST 14, 1994

Twenty-five years after turning down the offer of playing at Woodstock, Dylan takes part in the sequel, "Woodstock '94," in Saugerties, New York. He opens with *Jokerman*, and the rest of his 12-song set is filled with classics, including *All Along The Watchtower, Don't Think Twice, It's All Right, I Shall Be Released, Rainy Day Women #12 & 35*, and *It Ain't Me Babe.*"

25 Jahre, nachdem er es abgelehnt hatte, in Woodstock aufzutreten, nimmt Dylan an dem Festival „Woodstock '94" in Saugerties, New York, teil. Sein Eröffnungsstück ist *Jokerman*, die restlichen elf Stücke

sind lauter Klassiker: *All Along The Watchtower, Don't Think Twice, It's All Right, I Shall Be Released, Rainy Day Women #12 & 35* und *It Ain't Me Babe.*

Vingt-cinq ans après avoir décliné l'invitation à jouer à Woodstock, Dylan participe au concert anniversaire du grand événement, « Woodstock '94 », à Saugerties (New York). Il ouvre son set avec *Jokerman* avant de reprendre onze de ses titres les plus fameux, dont *All Along The Watchtower, Don't Think Twice, It's All Right, I Shall Be Released, Rainy Day Women #12 & 35* et *It Ain't Me Babe.*

THURSDAY, NOVEMBER 17 AND FRIDAY, NOVEMBER 18, 1994

Dylan tapes 23 songs for broadcast on an upcoming hour-long "MTV Unplugged" program at Sony's New York studios, with Pearl Jam's producer, Brendan O'Brien, on keyboards.

Dylan nimmt in den New Yorker Sony-Studios 23 Titel für die Reihe „MTV Unplugged" auf, mit dem Produzenten von Pearl Jam, Brendan O'Brien, am Keyboard.

Dylan enregistre 23 chansons pour l'émission « MTV Unplugged » aux studios Sony de New York, avec le producteur de Pearl Jam, Brendan O'Brien, aux claviers.

SATURDAY, SEPTEMBER 2, 1995

The Rock and Roll Hall of Fame Museum in Cleveland, Ohio, celebrates its opening with the all-star "Concert for the Hall of Fame" at Cleveland Stadium. Dylan performs *All Along The Watchtower, Just Like A Woman, Seeing The Real You At Last, Highway 61 Revisited*, and, with Bruce Springsteen, *Forever Young*.

Das Rock and Roll Hall of Fame Museum in Cleveland, Ohio, feiert seine Eröffnung mit dem All-Star-Event „Concert for the Hall of Fame" im Cleveland Stadium. Dylan spielt *All Along The Watchtower, Just Like A Woman, Seeing The Real You At Last, Highway 61 Revisited* und *Forever Young* mit Bruce Springsteen.

Le musée du Rock and Roll Hall of Fame de Cleveland (Ohio), fête son ouverture en organisant un concert dans le stade de la ville. Dylan joue *All Along The Watchtower, Just Like A Woman, Seeing The Real You At Last, Highway 61 Revisited* et *Forever Young* en duo avec Bruce Springsteen.

"By far the most haunting moments are provided by Bob Dylan, looking more ethereal than ever and singing an original work called Restless Farewell.*"*
„Den bewegendsten Moment verdanken wir Bob Dylan, der vergeistigter denn je wirkte und seinen frühen Song mit dem Titel Restless Farewell *sang."*
« Les moments les plus sensationnels nous ont sans doute été procurés par Bob Dylan, plus éthéré que jamais, qui chanta une composition originale intitulée Restless Farewell. *»*
THE NEW YORK TIMES - THE FRANK SINATRA TRIBUTE CONCERT

SUNDAY, NOVEMBER 19, 1995
Dylan joins Bruce Springsteen, Ray Charles, and others taking part in Frank Sinatra's 80th birthday tribute at the Shrine Auditorium. Dylan sings *Restless Farewell* at Sinatra's request. Two nights ago Dylan, Springsteen, Steve Lawrence, and Eydie Gormé gathered round a piano with Ol' Blue Eyes for an impromptu sing-along.

Dylan nimmt zusammen mit Bruce Springsteen, Ray Charles und anderen an der Hommage zum 80. Geburtstag von Frank Sinatra im Shrine Auditorium in L. A. teil. Dylan singt auf Sinatras Bitte *Restless Farewell*. Zwei Tage zuvor fanden sich Dylan, Springsteen, Steve Lawrence und Eydie Gormé mit Frank „Ol' Blue Eyes" Sinatra in einer spontanen Aktion zum Singen am Klavier zusammen.

Dylan participe, entre autres avec Bruce Springsteen et Ray Charles, à un concert donné pour les 80 ans de Frank Sinatra au Shrine Auditorium. À la demande de Sinatra, il chante *Restless Farewell*. Deux soirs plus tôt, Dylan, Springsteen, Steve Lawrence et Eydie Gormé se sont rassemblés autour d'un piano avec « Frankie les yeux bleus » pour un bœuf improvisé.

SATURDAY, JUNE 29, 1996
In the midst of another lengthy European tour and with Al Kooper and Ronnie Wood guesting, Dylan performs in the presence of HRH the Prince of Wales at the MasterCard Masters of Music Concert at London's Hyde Park in aid of the Prince's Trust charity.

Während einer weiteren ausgedehnten Europatournee mit Al Kooper und Ronnie Wood als Gaststars tritt Dylan beim MasterCard Masters of Music Concert im Londoner Hyde Park vor dem britischen Thronfolger Prinz Charles auf. Mit dem Konzert wird Geld für die Prince's Trust Charity gesammelt.

Au milieu d'une nouvelle tournée européenne de longue haleine avec Al Kooper et Ronnie Wood comme invités d'honneur, Dylan se produit à Hyde Park, à Londres, devant le prince Charles, lors du concert des MasterCard Masters of Music organisé au profit de l'œuvre de bienfaisance Prince's Trust.

MONDAY, JUNE 2, 1997

Upon Dylan's leaving the hospital, where he has been treated for histoplasmosis pericarditis—a fungal infection of the lung—Columbia Records issues the following statement: "Bob Dylan was released from the hospital this weekend where he had been undergoing medical tests and subsequent treatment for pericarditis brought on by histoplasmosis. He was admitted on May 25. Doctors are continuing to treat him and are confident that Mr. Dylan will make a full recovery in four to six weeks." He had already completed the recording of his new album, *Time Out Of Mind*, and had 25 more dates on his "Never Ending Tour."

Als Dylan aus dem Krankenhaus entlassen wird, wo er wegen Histoplasmose – einer Pilzinfektion der Lunge – behandelt wurde, veröffentlicht Columbia Records die folgende Presseerklärung: „Bob Dylan wurde an diesem Wochenende aus dem Krankenhaus entlassen, wo er sich medizinischen Untersuchungen unterzog. Die festgestellte Herzbeutelentzündung als Folge einer Histoplasmose wurde dort seit dem 25. Mai behandelt. Spezialisten betreuen ihn weiterhin und sind zuversichtlich, dass Mr. Dylan in vier bis sechs Wochen vollständig genesen sein wird." Zu diesem Zeitpunkt hat er die Aufnahmen zu einem neuen Album, *Time Out Of Mind*, bereits abgeschlossen, für seine „Never Ending Tour" stehen in diesem Jahr noch 25 Termine aus.

Alors que Dylan vient de quitter l'hôpital, où il a été traité pour une infection fongique des poumons, Columbia Records diffuse le communiqué suivant : « Bob Dylan est sorti ce week-end de l'hôpital, où il avait été admis le 25 mai. Des examens médicaux ont révélé une péricardite provoquée par une histoplasmose, que les médecins continuent à soigner. D'après eux, M. Dylan sera complètement remis dans quatre à six semaines. » Il a déjà terminé l'enregistrement de son nouvel album, *Time Out Of Mind*, mais son (interminable) Never Ending Tour comptait encore 25 dates.

"I'm just glad to be feeling better.
I really thought I'd be seeing Elvis soon."
„Ich bin nur froh, dass ich mich
besser fühle. Ich hatte wirklich gedacht,
ich würde demnächst Elvis sehen."
« Je suis vraiment content de me sentir mieux.
J'ai vraiment cru que j'allais bientôt voir Elvis. »
BOB DYLAN

*"I consider myself a poet first and a musician second.
I live like a poet and I'll die like a poet."*
*„Ich betrachte mich vor allem als Dichter und erst in zweiter
Linie als Musiker. Ich lebe wie ein Dichter, und ich werde auch
wie ein Dichter sterben."*
*« Je me considère d'abord comme un poète et ensuite comme
un musicien. Je vis comme un poète et je mourrai en poète. »*
**BOB DYLAN, ON BEING NOMINATED FOR
THE NOBEL PRIZE FOR LITERATURE**

SATURDAY, SEPTEMBER 27, 1997

Dylan performs *Knockin' On Heaven's Door*, *A Hard Rain's A-Gonna Fall*, and *Forever Young* for Pope John Paul II at a youth rally as part of the 23rd World Eucharistic Congress concert before 300,000 people at the fairgrounds in Bologna, Italy—an event broadcast live on Italian television. After *A Hard Rain's A-Gonna Fall*, Dylan and the Pontiff have a brief chat. Dylan was chosen for the event because—in the words of conference organizer, Monsignor Ernesto Vecchi—"he has a spiritual nature."

Dylan spielt vor Papst Johannes Paul II. und 300.000 jungen Leuten beim 23. Internationalen Eucharistischen Kongress auf dem Festplatz in Bologna *Knockin' On Heaven's Door*, *A Hard Rain's A-Gonna Fall* und *Forever Young* – das Ereignis wird im italienischen Fernsehen live übertragen. Nach *A Hard Rain's*

A-Gonna Fall führen Dylan und das Oberhaupt der katholischen Kirche ein kurzes Gespräch. Dylan wurde als Musiker für das Event ausgewählt, weil er – mit den Worten des Konferenzorganisators Monsignore Ernesto Vecchi – „ein spirituelles Wesen hat".

Dylan chante *Knockin' On Heaven's Door*, *A Hard Rain's A-Gonna Fall* et *Forever Young* pour le Pape Jean Paul II à l'occasion du 23e Congrès eucharistique mondial de la jeunesse, lors d'un concert qui rassemble 300 000 personnes à Bologne – un événement retransmis en direct par la télévision italienne. Après *A Hard Rain's A-Gonna Fall*, Dylan et le souverain pontife ont une brève entrevue. Dylan a été choisi parce que, selon les termes employés par l'organisateur de la conférence, Monseigneur Ernesto Vecchi, « il est de nature spirituelle ».

"People shouldn't take everything so literal.
Elvis sang: 'You ain't nothing but a hound dog.' It would
be very stupid to ask Elvis whether he was serious."
„Die Leute sollten nicht alles so wörtlich nehmen.
Elvis hat gesungen: ,You ain't nothing but a hound dog.'
(,Du bist nichts als ein Schürzenjäger.') Es wäre doch Quatsch,
Elvis fragen zu wollen, ob er das ernst gemeint hat."
« Les gens ne devraient pas tout prendre au pied de la
lettre. Elvis chantait : "Tu n'es rien d'autre qu'un chien errant"
("You ain't nothing but a hound dog"). Ce serait vraiment idiot
de demander à Elvis s'il était sérieux. »
BOB DYLAN, DER SPIEGEL, OCTOBER 1997

FRIDAY, NOVEMBER 14, 1997

Father and son appear onstage together for the first time when Dylan and his son Jakob's band, The Wall-flowers, perform at Applied Materials' 30th Anniversary Celebration, at the San Jose Civic Arena in San Jose, California. Of his son's musical career, Dylan said in a **USA Today** interview on September 26: "I'm proud of his accomplishments. He's still young and he's come a long way in a short time."

Vater und Sohn stehen zum ersten Mal zusammen auf der Bühne: Dylan spielt mit der Band seines Sohnes Jakob, The Wallflowers, bei einer geschlossenen Veranstaltung der Computerfirma Applied Materials, die ihr dreißigjähriges Bestehen in der San Jose Civic Arena in San Jose, Kalifornien, feiert. Dylan sagt der Zeitung **USA Today** am 26. September in einem Interview: „Ich bin stolz auf seine Leistungen. Er ist noch jung, hat aber in kurzer Zeit sehr viel erreicht."

Père et fils se produisent pour la première fois ensemble sur scène : Dylan se joint au groupe de son fils Jakob, The Wallflowers, lors d'une soirée privée donnée pour le 30ᵉ anniversaire de l'entreprise d'électronique Applied Materials, à la Civic Arena de San Jose (Californie). Le 26 septembre, Dylan a commenté la carrière musicale de son fils dans une interview à **USA Today** : « Je suis fier de ce qu'il a accompli. Il est encore jeune et il a parcouru un long chemin en peu de temps. »

SUNDAY, DECEMBER 7, 1997

Dylan is a recipient, with Jessye Norman, Lauren Bacall, Edward Villella, and Charlton Heston, of the Kennedy Center Honors Lifetime Award at the 20th annual ceremonies in Washington. Gregory Peck, in his introduction, says, "When I was a little kid in La Jolla, California, which is a very small town, we had a parade on the 4th of July and I remember clearly the sight of Civil War veterans marching down the main street, kicking up the dust. The first time I heard Bob Dylan, it brought back that memory. And I thought of him as something of a Civil War type. Some time ago I bought a new Dylan album and I was listening to a song called *Brownsville Girl* and I heard these lines: 'There was a movie I seen one time. I think I saw it through twice. It starred Gregory Peck. He wore a gun and was shot in the back. I just can't get it out of my head.' Dylan was singing about a picture that I made called 'The Gun-fighter' about the lone man in town with people comin' in to kill him and everybody wants him out of town before the shooting starts. When I met Bob, years later, I told him that meant a lot to me and the best way I could sum him up is to say—Bob Dylan has never been about to get out of town before the shootin' starts. Thank you, Mr. Dylan, for rocking the country and the ages."

Dylan nimmt zusammen mit Jessye Norman, Lauren Bacall, Edward Villella und Charlton Heston den

Kennedy Center Honors Lifetime Award in Washington entgegen. Gregory Peck sagt in seiner Laudatio: „Als ich ein Kind war in La Jolla, Kalifornien, einem sehr kleinen Ort, gab es bei uns am Unabhängigkeitstag eine Parade, und ich kann mich noch genau an den Anblick der Bürgerkriegsveteranen erinnern, die die Hauptstraße entlangmarschierten und den Staub aufwirbelten. Als ich Bob Dylan zum ersten Mal hörte, brachte das diese Erinnerungen zurück, und ich stellte ihn mir als eine Figur aus dem Bürgerkrieg vor. Vor einiger Zeit habe ich mir ein neues Dylan-Album gekauft, darauf war ein Lied, das hieß *Brownsville Girl* und ich hörte die Zeilen: ‚There was a movie I seen one time. I think I saw it through twice. It starred Gregory Peck. He wore a gun und was shot in the back. I just can't get it out of my head.' Dylans Song handelte von einem Film mit mir, ‚Der Scharfschütze', der die Geschichte eines Einzelgängers erzählt, zu dem die Leute in die Stadt kommen, um ihn zu ermorden, und alle in der Stadt wollen ihn loswerden, bevor die Schießerei anfängt. Als ich Bob Jahre später kennenlernte, sage ich ihm, wie viel mir diese Textzeile bedeutet. Ich kann es eigentlich nur so zusammenfassen – Bob Dylan war nie darauf bedacht, sich aus dem Staub zu machen, bevor die Schießerei losgeht. Danke, Mr. Dylan, dass Sie im ganzen Land und bei allen Altersgruppen für Aufruhr sorgen."

Vingtième cérémonie des Kennedy Center Honors, à Washington : Dylan fait partie, avec Jessye Norman, Lauren Bacall, Edward Villella et Charlton Heston, des lauréats du Lifetime Award. Son prix lui est remis par Gregory Peck, qui l'annonce ainsi : « Quand j'étais enfant, à La Jolla, une très petite ville de Californie, il y avait une parade pour le 4 juillet et je garde une image très nette des vétérans de la guerre de Sécession qui défilaient sur l'avenue principale, foulant la poussière. La première fois que j'ai entendu Bob Dylan, cette parade m'est revenue en mémoire. Il y a un petit moment, j'ai acheté un nouvel album de Dylan ; j'écoutais la chanson *Brownsville Girl* et j'ai entendu ces phrases : "J'ai vu un film, un jour. Je crois même que je l'ai vu deux fois. C'était avec Gregory Peck. Il portait une arme et se faisait tirer dans le dos. Je n'arrive pas à me l'enlever de la tête." Dylan parlait d'un film que j'avais tourné, "La Cible humaine", où un homme solitaire attend les hommes venus pour le tuer alors que tous les habitants de la ville tentent de le chasser avant le début de la fusillade. Quand j'ai rencontré Bob, bien des années plus tard, je lui ai dit combien son hommage m'avait touché, et la meilleure façon dont je peux le résumer, c'est en disant que Bob Dylan n'a jamais quitté la ville avant le début de la fusillade. Merci, M. Dylan, d'avoir bousculé le pays avec tant de constance. »

SATURDAY, JANUARY 17, 1998

Stanford University holds a symposium in the Kresge Auditorium, addressing such topics as "Only A Pawn In Their Game: Bob Dylan And Politics" and "The Sound Of One Dog Barking: Bob Dylan And Religious Experience." More than 400 people attend the conference, which features the opinions of **Crawdaddy!** editor Paul Williams, Whiting Fellow Tino Markworth, and Christopher Ricks, professor in the core curriculum at Boston University.

An der Stanford University findet im Kresge Auditorium ein Symposium über Dylan statt, mit Vorträgen wie „Only A Pawn In Their Game: Bob Dylan und die Politik" und „Der Klang eines bellenden Hundes: Bob Dylan und religiöse Erfahrungen". Über 400 Leute nehmen an der Konferenz teil, auf der Paul Williams (Herausgeber der Zeitschrift **Crawdaddy!**), Tino Markworth (Whiting Fellow) und Christopher Ricks (Boston University) Vorträge halten.

L'université de Stanford organise dans son auditorium Kresge un symposium autour de thèmes comme « Juste un pion dans leur jeu : Bob Dylan et la politique » ou « Un chien qui aboie : Bob Dylan et l'expérience religieuse ». Plus de 400 personnes assistent aux conférences données par Paul Williams, le rédacteur-en-chef de **Crawdaddy!**, Tino Markworth, professeur à Stanford, et Christopher Ricks, professeur permanent de l'université de Boston.

WEDNESDAY, FEBRUARY 25, 1998

At the 40th annual Grammy Awards, Michael Portnoy rushes onstage during Dylan's performance of *Love Sick* and "dances" alongside the unfazed legend, baring the words Soy Bomb on his naked chest. The 26-year-old describes himself as a "multigenre mastermind artist." Dylan wins three awards—Album of the Year, Best Contemporary Folk Album *(Time Out Of Mind)*, and Best Rock Vocal Performance, Male *(Cold Irons Bound)*—while son Jakob wins a pair— Best Rock Song for *One Headlight* and Best Rock Performance by a Duo or Group with Vocal for The Wallflowers.

Bei der 40. Grammy-Verleihung springt Michael Portnoy auf die Bühne, während Dylan *Love Sick* singt, und tanzt neben der völlig unbeeindruckten Ikone herum; auf seiner entblößten Brust steht Soy Bomb. Der 26-Jährige beschreibt sich als „Multigenre-Mastermind-Künstler". Dylan gewinnt in drei Kategorien: „Album des Jahres", „Bestes zeitgenössisches Folkal-

bum" *(Time Out Of Mind)* und „Beste männliche Gesangsdarbietung – Rock" *(Cold Irons Bound)*. Sein Sohn Jakob gewinnt in zwei Kategorien: „Bester Rocksong" für *One Headlight* und „Beste Darbietung eines Duos oder einer Gruppe mit Gesang – Rock" für The Wallflowers.

Quarantième cérémonie annuelle des Grammy Awards. Michael Portnoy se précipite sur scène pendant que Dylan chante *Love Sick*, et se met à « danser » à côté de la légende, médusée, les mots « Soy Bomb » inscrits sur son torse nu. Le jeune homme de 26 ans se décrit comme un « artiste cérébral multigenre ». Dylan remporte trois prix – Album de l'année, Meilleur album folk contemporain *(Time Out Of Mind)* et Meilleure performance vocale masculine, catégorie rock *(Cold Irons Bound)* – tandis que son fils Jakob en reçoit deux – Meilleure chanson, catégorie Rock, pour *One Headlight* et Meilleure performance rock par un duo ou un groupe avec voix pour The Wallflowers.

TUESDAY, MARCH 2, 1999

Dylan helps launch the newest House of Blues venue at Las Vegas' Mandalay Bay Resort & Casino, with a performance highlighted by U2 singer Bono joining him on *Knockin' On Heaven's Door* for an encore.

Dylan tritt bei den Feierlichkeiten zur Einweihung des „House of Blues" im Mandalay Bay Resort & Casino in Las Vegas auf. Stargast Bono von U2 gesellt sich zu ihm und singt mit ihm zusammen *Knockin' On Heaven's Door* als Zugabe.

Dylan inaugure la Maison du Blues, la dernière attraction du Mandalay Bay Resort & Casino de Las Vegas ; pour le rappel, le chanteur de U2, Bono, chante avec lui *Knockin' On Heaven's Door*.

WEDNESDAY, JUNE 30, 1999

Following an appearance at the "All-Star Tribute to Johnny Cash" in April and a tour with Paul Simon (at the opening show, they sang *The Sounds Of Silence, I Walk The Line/Blue Moon Of Kentucky*, and *Forever Young* together), Dylan takes part in "Eric Clapton & Friends," a benefit concert at Madison Square Garden, raising money for Clapton's drug and alcohol rehab facility, Crossroads Centre, in Antigua. Clapton joins Dylan on three of his numbers, and fellow participant

Sheryl Crow joins in on vocals and accordion on *Bright Lights, Big City*.

Nach einem Auftritt beim „All-Star Tribute to Johnny Cash" im April und einer Tournee mit Paul Simon (beim ersten Konzert singen sie zusammen *The Sounds Of Silence, I Walk The Line/Blue Moon Of Kentucky* und *Forever Young*) nimmt Dylan am Benefizkonzert „Eric Clapton & Friends" im Madison Square Garden teil, dessen Einnahmen Claptons Alkohol- und Drogenentzugseinrichtung Crossroads Centre in Antigua zugutekommen. Clapton kommt bei drei Stücken zu Dylan auf die Bühne, Sheryl Crow steuert Gesang und Akkordeon zu *Bright Lights, Big City* bei.

Après une apparition, en avril, au « All-Star Tribute to Johnny Cash » et une tournée avec Paul Simon (lors du concert inaugural, ils chantent ensemble *The Sounds Of Silence, I Walk The Line/Blue Moon Of Kentucky* et *Forever Young*), Dylan participe au concert de bienfaisance « Eric Clapton & Friends », au Madison Square Garden, au profit du Crossroads Centre, établissement de désintoxication ouvert par Clapton à Antigua. Clapton se joint à Dylan pour trois chansons et Sheryl Crow l'accompagne de sa voix et à l'accordéon sur *Bright Lights, Big City*.

THE 2000^S

SEIT 2000

LES ANNÉES 2000

MONDAY, MAY 15, 2000

Dylan receives the prestigious Polar Music Prize from Swedish King Carl XVI Gustaf at Stockholm's Berwaldhallen. The committee's citation reads: "Bob Dylan's influence, as a singer-songwriter, on the development of 20th-century popular music is indisputable. His achievements encompass almost four decades of constantly changing modes of creativity, always innovative, but always based on American musical traditions and roots. Starting with folk music and reaching the heights of critical and public fame, he set aside the rules of the day, appearing no longer alone with his acoustic guitar, but in the company of a rock and roll band. It was a development that required both integrity and determination, a move that cemented his role as one of the greatest rock artists of our time. Bob Dylan's ability to combine poetry, harmony, and melody in a meaningful, often provocative context has captivated millions in all age groups, and in most cultures and societies. Through his modest, persuasive musical approach, he has demonstrated an impressive ability to question the most determined political forces, to fight all forms of prejudice, and to offer unflinching support for the less fortunate. Even those who might not have shared his views would find it impossible to argue against Bob Dylan's musical and poetic brilliance."

Dylan nimmt den inoffiziellen „Nobelpreis für Musik", den Polar Music Prize, aus der Hand von König Carl XVI. Gustaf von Schweden in den Stockholmer Berwaldhallen entgegen. In der Laudatio des Komitees heißt es: „Bob Dylans Einfluss als Singer-Songwriter auf die Entwicklung der Populärmusik im 20. Jahrhundert ist unumstritten. Er ist seit fast vier Jahrzehnten wandlungsfähig in seiner Kreativität, seine Leistungen sind stets innovativ und bewahren dabei immer den Bezug zu den Wurzeln amerikanischer Musiktradition. Er begann als Folkmusiker und erntete höchste Anerkennung bei Kritik und Publikum. Er setzte sich über die Erwartungen seiner Zeitgenossen hinweg und trat nicht länger mit seiner akustischen Gitarre, sondern in Begleitung einer Rock and Roll Band auf. Es war eine Entwicklung, die sowohl Integrität als auch Zielstrebigkeit verlangte, eine Entscheidung, die seine Rolle als einer der größten Rockmusiker unserer Zeit festigte. Bob Dylans Fähigkeiten, Poesie, Harmonie und Melodie in einem aussagekräftigen und oft provokanten Kontext miteinander zu kombinieren, begeistert Millionen von Hörern aller Altersgruppen in vielen Ländern und Kulturen. Durch seine bescheidene, überzeugende musikalische Herangehensweise hat er auf beeindruckende Weise die Fähigkeit demonstriert, selbst stärkste politische Kräfte zu hinterfragen, alle Arten von Vorurteilen zu bekämpfen und den Benachteiligten der Gesellschaft unbeirrt Unterstützung zukommen zu lassen. Selbst diejenigen, die nicht mit Bob Dylans Ansichten übereinstimmen, können seine Brillanz als Musiker und Dichter nicht leugnen.

Le roi Carl XVI Gustaf de Suède décerne à Dylan le prestigieux prix Polar Music, à la Berwaldhallen de Stockholm. Le jury motive son choix ainsi : « L'influence de Bob Dylan sur le développement de la musique populaire au XXᵉ siècle est indiscutable. Il a notamment réussi, en près de quarante ans de carrière, à constamment faire évoluer son travail créatif tout en le fondant

toujours sur les traditions et les racines musicales américaines. Il a commencé par la musique folk et atteint les sommets du succès critique et populaire, puis il a délaissé la tendance du moment, n'est plus apparu seul sur scène avec sa guitare, mais en compagnie d'un groupe de rock and roll. C'était un changement qui réclamait intégrité et détermination, un geste qui a assis son personnage et l'a fait entrer au panthéon des plus grands musiciens rock de notre époque. La manière dont Bob Dylan combine poésie, harmonie et mélodie et crée une œuvre riche de sens et souvent provocatrice captive des millions de personnes de tous les âges, dans la plupart des cultures et des sociétés. Par son approche musicale modeste et persuasive, il a démontré une impressionnante capacité de remise en question des forces politiques les plus déterminées et une immense aptitude à la lutte contre toutes les formes d'injustice, et n'a jamais cessé de soutenir les populations défavorisées. Même ceux qui ne partagent pas ses idées ne peuvent mettre en doute les dons de musicien et de poète de Bob Dylan. »

SUNDAY, MARCH 25, 2001
Things Have Changed, from the movie "Wonder Boys," wins the Oscar for Best Song at the 73rd annual Academy Awards. Dylan performs the song live by satellite from Australia, where he is currently on tour. On receiving the prize, he says: "Oh good God, this is amazing ... And I want to thank the members of the Academy who, who were bold enough to, to give me this award for this song, which obviously, a song that doesn't pussyfoot around nor turn a blind eye to human nature. And God bless you all with peace, tranquility, and good will. Thanks."

Für *Things Have Changed* aus dem Film „Wonder Boys" gewinnt Dylan den Oscar für den „Besten Song". Dylan spielt das Lied live über Satellit in Australien, wo er gerade auf Tour ist. Zur Verleihung des Academy Awards sagt er: „Gütiger Gott, das ist ein Wunder ... und ich möchte mich auch bei den Academy-Mitgliedern bedanken, die den Mut hatten, mir den Oscar für diesen Song zuzusprechen, bei dem ich kein Blatt vor den Mund genommen und nichts an der menschlichen Natur beschönigt habe. Gott segne Sie und gebe Ihnen Frieden, innere Ruhe und einen guten Willen. Danke."

Things Have Changed, qui fait partie de la bande originale du film « Wonder Boys », remporte l'oscar de la Meilleure chanson lors de la 73ᵉ cérémonie des Academy Awards. Dylan joue sa chanson en duplex d'Australie, où il est en tournée. « Oh bon Dieu, c'est incroyable, déclare-t-il... Je tiens à remercier les membres de l'Académie, ont eu le courage de me donner ce prix pour cette chanson, qui, à l'évidence, ne fait pas de ronds de jambe et ne s'aveugle pas devant la nature humaine. Dieu puisse vous apporter à tous paix, tranquillité et bonne volonté. Merci. »

SATURDAY, AUGUST 3, 2002

After a 37-year absence, Dylan returns to the Newport Folk Festival, now known as the Apple & Eve Newport Folk Festival—the times they are indeed a-changing. For some reason, he decides to perform wearing a fake beard and fake hair. During the year, he will play a relatively meager 107 shows, mainly due to filming "Masked And Anonymous," which he writes with veteran comedy scribe Larry Charles.

Nach 37 Jahren kehrt Dylan zum Newport Folk Festival zurück, das mittlerweile Apple & Eve Newport Folk Festival heißt – „the times they are a-changing ..." Aus unbekannten Gründen tritt er mit angeklebtem Bart und Perücke auf. In diesem Jahr spielt er bei „nur" 107 Konzerten – für ihn relativ wenig – hauptsächlich wegen der Dreharbeiten zu dem Film „Masked And Anonymous", den er zusammen mit dem altgedienten Komödienautor Larry Charles geschrieben hat.

Après 37 ans d'absence, Dylan participe à nouveau au Festival folk de Newport, rebaptisé « Apple & Eve Newport Folk Festival » – les temps changent, décidément. Il décide, pour une raison obscure, de porter une fausse barbe et une perruque. Cette année-là, il ne donne « que » 107 concerts, principalement parce qu'il tourne « Masked And Anonymous », coécrit avec le vétéran de la comédie Larry Charles.

WEDNESDAY, JUNE 23, 2004

In Scotland, University of St. Andrews' chancellor Sir Kenneth Dover presents Dylan with an honorary degree as Doctor of Music.

Sir Kenneth Dover, Kanzler der University of St. Andrews in Schottland, ernennt Dylan zum Ehrendoktor der Musik.

Sir Kenneth Dover, le président de l'université St. Andrews, en Écosse, nomme Dylan docteur honoris causa en musique.

"Chancellor, in recognition of his incomparable contribution to musical and literary culture, I invite you to confer on Bob Dylan the Degree of Doctor of Music, honoris causa."

„Herr Kanzler, ich bitte Sie nun, Bob Dylan in Anerkennung seines beispiellosen Beitrags zur Musik und zur Literatur den Rang eines Doktors der Musik, honoris causa, zu verleihen."

« Président, en reconnaissance de son inestimable contribution à la culture musicale et littéraire, je vous invite à décerner à Monsieur Dylan la distinction de Docteur en musique honoris causa. »

PROFESSOR NEIL CORCORAN

MONDAY, SEPTEMBER 26 AND TUESDAY, SEPTEMBER 27, 2005

Martin Scorsese-lensed two-part documentary covering Dylan's career from 1961 to 1966, "No Direction Home," airs on PBS and the BBC. The lauded film will win Emmy, Grammy, and Television Critics Association awards.

Martin Scorseses zweiteiliger Dokumentarfilm „No Direction Home" wird von PBS und der BBC ausgestrahlt. Der viel gelobte Fernsehfilm, der Dylans Karriere von 1961 bis 1966 nachzeichnet, wird mit einem Emmy, einem Grammy und weiteren Frensehpreisen ausgezeichnet.

«No Direction Home», le documentaire en deux parties réalisé par Martin Scorsese et retraçant la carrière de Bob Dylan entre 1961 et 1966, est diffusé sur les chaînes de télévision PBS et la BBC. Salué par la critique, le film est distingué par les jurys des Emmy et des Grammy Awards, ainsi que par l'Association des critiques de télévision.

WEDNESDAY, MAY 3, 2006

In an ever-evolving career, Dylan begins hosting an eclectic, hour-long weekly radio show called "The Theme Time Radio Hour" on XM Satellite Radio. Each program follows a theme, the inaugural show being about weather, and including music from artists as diverse as Muddy Waters, Stevie Wonder, Judy Garland, and Frank Sinatra. His baseball program will be added to the archive of the National Baseball Hall of Fame Library.

Seiner stets verwandlungsreichen Karriere als Künstler fügt Dylan eine weitere Facette hinzu: Auf XM Satellite Radio moderiert er einmal wöchentlich eine ausgefallene, einstündige Sendung mit dem Titel „The Theme Time Radio Hour". Jedes der einstündigen Programme dreht sich um ein bestimmtes Thema, in der Auftaktsendung geht es um das Wetter, die Musik kommt von so unterschiedlichen Sängern wie Muddy Waters, Stevie Wonder, Judy Garland und Frank Sinatra. Seine Sendung über Baseball wird in das Bibliotheksarchiv der National Baseball Hall of Fame aufgenommen.

Nouvelle étape dans une carrière en constante évolution : Dylan présente une émission hebdomadaire éclectique d'une heure, « The Theme Time Radio Hour », sur la station de radio XM Satellite. Il la consacre chaque semaine à un sujet différent. Le thème de la première est la météo, illustré en musique par des artistes aussi divers que Muddy Waters, Stevie Wonder, Judy Garland ou Frank Sinatra. Son émission sur le base-ball sera versée aux archives de la bibliothèque du National Baseball Hall of Fame.

FRIDAY, AUGUST 31, 2007

Inspired, as the credits say, "by the music and many lives of Bob Dylan," Todd Haynes' movie "I'm Not There," starring Cate Blanchett, is launched at the Telluride Film Festival.

Todd Haynes Film „I'm Not There", der, wie es im Abspann heißt, „von der Musik und den vielen Leben Bob Dylans inspiriert wurde, hat mit Cate Blanchett in der Hauptrolle beim Telluride Film Festival Premiere.

Inspiré, d'après le générique, « par la musique et les nombreuses vies de Bob Dylan », le film de Todd Haynes « I'm Not There », avec Cate Blanchett dans le rôle principal, est présenté au Festival du film de Telluride.

"Dylan's own songs ... seem to be the strongest influence on this brilliantly strange, often funny, and ultimately heartbreaking film."
„Dylans eigene Songs [...] scheinen diesen seltsamen, oft witzigen und letztendlich tieftraurigen Film am stärksten beeinflusst zu haben."
« Les propres chansons de Dylan... semblent être la source d'inspiration la plus forte de ce film si étrangement brillant, souvent drôle et, au bout du compte, bouleversant. »
DAVID GATES, NEWSWEEK

MONDAY, APRIL 7, 2008

Dylan's son Jesse receives a Special Citation in Music on behalf of his father from the Pulitzer Prize Board, citing "his profound impact on popular music and American culture, marked by lyrical compositions of extraordinary poetic power." Prize administrator Sig Gissler said that the award reflected the efforts of the Pulitzer board to broaden the scope of the music prize, and encompass the full range of excellence in American music. It also recognizes Mr. Dylan's lyrical compositions of extraordinary poetic power.

Dylans Sohn Jesse nimmt für seinen Vater vom Pulitzer-Komitee einen Sonderpreis für Musik entgegen. Dylan erhält den Preis für den „weitreichenden Einfluss seiner lyrischen Kompositionen von außerordentlicher dichterischer Kraft auf die Populärmusik und amerikanische Kultur". Der Vorsitzende des Ko-

mitees Sig Gissler betont, der Preis reflektiere die Bemuhungen des Pulitzer-Komitees, die Reichweite des Musikpreises zu erweitern und die gesamte Bandbreite hervorragender Leistungen in der amerikanischen Musik zu berücksichtigen.

Jesse Dylan reçoit au nom de son père une citation spéciale en musique décernée par le jury du Prix Pulitzer, lequel rend hommage à «l'impact profond [de Bob Dylan] sur la musique populaire et la culture américaine, et ses compositions lyriques d'une puissance poétique extraordinaire». Le président du jury, Sig Gissler, déclare que cette récompense reflète la volonté du jury du Pulitzer d'élargir le registre du Prix afin d'embrasser la musique américaine dans toute son excellence.

FRIDAY, JUNE 6, 2008

In an interview given to **The Times'** Alan Jackson a week ago in Odense, Denmark, Dylan tells Jackson that the United States is in a state of upheaval. "Poverty is demoralizing. You can't expect people to have the virtue of purity when they are poor. But we've got this guy out there now who is redefining the nature of politics from the ground up ... Barack Obama. He's redefining what a politician is, so we'll have to see how things play out. Am I hopeful? Yes, I'm hopeful that things might change. Some things are going to have to."

In der Londoner **Times** erscheint ein Interview, das Dylan eine Woche zuvor dem Journalisten Alan Jackson in Odense, Dänemark, gegeben hat. Dylan bringt darin die Überzeugung zum Ausdruck, dass die USA sich in einer Phase des Umbruchs befinden. „Armut ist demoralisierend. Man kann nicht erwarten, dass Leute sich moralisch vorbildhaft verhalten, wenn sie arm sind. Aber wir haben jetzt einen Mann, der das Wesen

der Politik von Grund auf neu definiert: Barack Obama. Er bietet eine neue Definition dafür, was ein Politiker ist, wir müssen also abwarten, wie sich die Dinge entwickeln. Ob ich Hoffnung habe? Ja, ich habe die Hoffnung, dass die Lage sich verändern wird. Viele Dinge werden sich ändern müssen."

Dans une interview accordée une semaine plus tôt au journaliste du **Times** Alan Jackson à Odense, au Danemark, Dylan déclare que les États-Unis sont au bord de l'insurrection. « La pauvreté est désespérante. Il ne faut pas s'attendre à ce que les gens soient purs et vertueux quand ils sont pauvres. Mais maintenant, nous avons ce gars qui redéfinit la nature de la politique de fond en comble : Barack Obama. Il redéfinit le rôle du politicien, donc il va falloir attendre de voir comment les choses vont finir. Si j'ai de l'espoir ? Oui, j'ai l'espoir que les choses changent. Certaines choses vont devoir changer. »

3
ESSENTIAL RECORDINGS

DIE WICHTIGSTEN ALBEN

PRINCIPAUX ENREGISTREMENTS

BOB DYLAN (1962)

1 You're No Good 2 Talkin' New York 3 In My Time Of Dyin' 4 Man Of Constant Sorrow 5 Fixin' To Die 6 Pretty Peggy-O 7 Highway 51 Blues 8 Gospel Plow 9 Baby Let Me Follow You Down 10 House Of The Risin' Sun 11 Freight Train Blues 12 Song To Woody 13 See That My Grave Is Kept Clean

THE FREEWHEELIN' BOB DYLAN (1963)

1 Blowin' In The Wind 2 Girl From The North Country 3 Masters Of War 4 Down The Highway 5 Bob Dylan's Blues 6 A Hard Rain's A-Gonna Fall 7 Don't Think Twice, It's All Right 8 Bob Dylan's Dream 9 Oxford Town 10 Talkin' World War III Blues 11 Corrina, Corrina 12 Honey, Just Allow Me One More Chance 13 I Shall Be Free

THE TIMES THEY ARE A-CHANGIN' (1964)

1 The Times They Are A-Changin' 2 Ballad Of Hollis Brown 3 With God On Our Side 4 One Too Many Mornings 5 North Country Blues 6 Only A Pawn In Their Game 7 Boots Of Spanish Leather 8 When The Ship Comes In 9 The Lonesome Death Of Hattie Carroll 10 Restless Farewell

ANOTHER SIDE OF BOB DYLAN (1964)

1 All I Really Want To Do 2 Black Crow Blues 3 Spanish Harlem Incident 4 Chimes Of Freedom 5 I Shall Be Free No. 10 6 To Ramona 7 Motorpsycho Nitemare 8 My Back Pages 9 I Don't Believe You (She Acts Like We Never Have Met) 10 Ballad In Plain D 11 It Ain't Me Babe

BRINGING IT ALL BACK HOME (1965)

1 Subterranean Homesick Blues 2 She Belongs To Me 3 Maggie's Farm 4 Love Minus Zero 5 Outlaw Blues 6 On The Road Again 7 Bob Dylan's 115th Dream 8 Mr. Tambourine Man 9 Gates Of Eden 10 It's Alright, Ma (I'm Only Bleeding) 11 It's All Over Now, Baby Blue

HIGHWAY 61 REVISITED (1965)

1 Like A Rolling Stone 2 Tombstone Blues 3 It Takes A Lot To Laugh, It Takes A Train To Cry 4 From A Buick 6 5 Ballad Of A Thin Man 6 Queen Jane Approximately 7 Highway 61 Revisited 8 Just Like Tom Thumb's Blues 9 Desolation Row

"... an insane rush of ideas ... a sound like a cold dagger in the brain ... a shimmering presence of something divine ... Tunes, tunes, tunes ... Dylan the tunesmith never had better days than these."

Q ON BLONDE ON BLONDE

BLONDE ON BLONDE (1966)
1 Rainy Day Women #12 & 35 **2** Pledging My Time **3** Visions Of Johanna **4** One Of Us Must Know (Sooner Or Later) **5** I Want You **6** Stuck Inside Of Mobile With The Memphis Blues Again **7** Leopard-Skin Pill-Box Hat **8** Just Like A Woman **9** Most Likely You Go Your Way (And I'll Go Mine) **10** Temporary Like Achilles **11** Absolutely Sweet Marie **12** Fourth Time Around **13** Obviously Five Believers **14** Sad-Eyed Lady Of The Lowlands

JOHN WESLEY HARDING (1967)
1 John Wesley Harding **2** As I Went Out One Morning **3** I Dreamed I Saw St. Augustine **4** All Along The Watchtower **5** The Ballad Of Frankie Lee And Judas Priest **6** Drifter's Escape **7** Dear Landlord **8** I Am A Lonesome Hobo **9** I Pity The Poor Immigrant **10** The Wicked Messenger **11** Down Along The Cove **12** I'll Be Your Baby Tonight

NASHVILLE SKYLINE (1969)
1 Girl From The North Country **2** Nashville Skyline Rag **3** To Be Alone With You **4** I Threw It All Away **5** Peggy Day **6** Lay Lady Lay **7** One More Night **8** Tell Me That It Isn't True **9** Country Pie **10** Tonight I'll Be Staying Here With You

NEW MORNING (1970)
1 If Not For You **2** Day Of The Locusts **3** Time Passes Slowly **4** Went To See The Gypsy **5** Winterlude **6** If Dogs Run Free **7** New Morning **8** Sign On The Window **9** One More Weekend **10** Man In Me **11** Three Angels **12** Father Of Night

PAT GARRETT & BILLY THE KID (1973)
1 Main Title Theme (Billy) **2** Cantina Theme (Workin' For The Law) **3** Billy 1 **4** Bunkhouse Theme **5** River Theme **6** Turkey Chase **7** Knockin' On Heaven's Door **8** Final Theme **9** Billy 4 **10** Billy 7

PLANET WAVES (1974)
1 On A Night Like This 2 Going, Going, Gone 3 Tough Mama 4 Hazel 5 Something There Is About You 6 Forever Young 7 Forever Young 8 Dirge 9 You Angel You 10 Never Say Goodbye 11 Wedding Song

BEFORE THE FLOOD (1974)
1 Most Likely You Go Your Way (And I'll Go Mine) 2 Lay Lady Lay 3 Rainy Day Women #12 & 35 4 Knockin' On Heaven's Door 5 It Ain't Me, Babe 6 Ballad Of A Thin Man 7 Up On Cripple Creek 8 I Shall Be Released 9 Endless Highway 10 The Night They Drove Old Dixie Down 11 Stage Fright 12 Don't Think Twice, It's All Right 13 Just Like A Woman 14 It's Alright, Ma (I'm Only Bleeding) 15 The Shape I'm In 16 When You Awake 17 The Weight 18 All Along The Watchtower 19 Highway 61 Revisited 20 Like A Rolling Stone 21 Blowin' In The Wind

BLOOD ON THE TRACKS (1975)
1 Tangled Up In Blue 2 Simple Twist Of Fate 3 You're A Big Girl Now 4 Idiot Wind 5 You're Gonna Make Me Lonesome When You Go 6 Meet Me In The Morning 7 Lily, Rosemary And The Jack Of Hearts 8 If You See Her, Say Hello 9 Shelter From The Storm 10 Buckets Of Rain

THE BASEMENT TAPES (1975)
1 Odds And Ends 2 Orange Juice Blues 3 Million Dollar Bash 4 Yazoo Street Scandal 5 Goin' To Acapulco 6 Katie' Been Gone 7 Lo And Behold! 8 Bessie Smith 9 Clothes Line Saga 10 Apple Suckling Tree 11 Please, Mrs. Henry 12 Tears Of Rage 13 Too Much Of Nothing 14 Yea! Heavy And A Bottle Of Bread 15 Ain't No More Cane 16 Crash On The Levee 17 Ruben Remus 18 Tiny Montgomery 19 You Ain't Goin' Nowhere 20 Don't Ya Tell Henry 21 Nothing Was Delivered 22 Open The Door, Homer 23 Long Distance Operater 24 This Wheel's On Fire

DESIRE (1976)
1 Hurricane 2 Isis 3 Mozambique
4 One More Cup Of Coffee
5 Oh, Sister 6 Joey 7 Romance In
Durango 8 Black Diamond Bay
9 Sara

STREET LEGAL (1978)
1 Changing Of The Guards
2 New Pony 3 No Time To Think
4 Baby, Stop Crying 5 Is Your
Love In Vain? 6 Señor (Tales Of
Yankee Power) 7 True Love Tends
To Forget 8 We Better Talk This
Over 9 Where Are You Tonight?
(Journey Through Dark Heat)

**SLOW TRAIN COMING
(1979)**
1 Gotta Serve Somebody
2 Precious Angel 3 I Believe In
You 4 Slow Train 5 Gonna Change
My Way Of Thinking 6 Do Right
To Me Baby (Do Unto Others)
7 When You Gonna Wake Up
8 Man Gave Names To All The
Animals 9 When He Returns

INFIDELS (1983)
1 Jokerman 2 Sweetheart Like
You 3 Neighborhood Bully
4 License To Kill 5 Man Of Peace
6 Union Sundown 7 I And I
8 Don't Fall Apart On Me Tonight

EMPIRE BURLESQUE (1985)
1 Tight Connection To My Heart
(Has Anyone Seen My Love?)
2 Seeing The Real You At Last
3 I'll Remember You 4 Clean Cut
Kid 5 Never Gonna Be The Same
Again 6 Trust Yourself
7 Emotionally Yours 8 When The
Night Comes Falling From The
Sky 9 Something's Burning, Baby
10 Dark Eyes

OH MERCY (1989)
1 Political World 2 Where
Teardrops Fall 3 Everything Is
Broken 4 Ring Them Bells
5 Man In The Long Black Coat
6 Most Of The Time 7 What
Good Am I? 8 Disease Of
Conceit 9 What Was It You
Wanted 10 Shooting Star

GOOD AS I BEEN TO YOU (1992)
1 Frankie And Albert 2 Jim Jones 3 Black Jack Davey 4 Canadee-I-O 5 Sitting On Top Of The World 6 Little Maggie 7 Hard Times 8 Step It Up And Go 9 Tomorrow Night 10 Arthur McBride 11 You're Gonna Quit Me 12 Diamond Joe 13 Froggie Went A-Courtin'

WORLD GONE WRONG (1993)
1 World Gone Wrong 2 Love Henry 3 Ragged & Dirty 4 Blood In My Eyes 5 Broke Down Engine 6 Delia 7 Stack A Lee 8 Two Soldiers 9 Jack-A-Roe 10 Lone Pilgrim

TIME OUT OF MIND (1997)
1 Love Sick 2 Dirt Road Blues 3 Standing In The Doorway 4 Million Miles 5 Trying To Get To Heaven 6 'Til I Fell In Love With You 7 Not Dark Yet 8 Cold Irons Bound 9 Make You Feel My Love 10 Can't Wait 11 Highlands

LOVE AND THEFT (2001)
1 Tweedle Dee & Tweedle Dum 2 Mississippi 3 Summer Days 4 Bye And Bye 5 Lonesome Day Blues 6 Floater (Too Much To Ask) 7 High Water (For Charley Patton) 8 Moonlight 9 Honest With Me 10 Po' Boy 11 Cry A While 12 Sugar Baby

MODERN TIMES (2006)
1 Thunder On The Mountain 2 Spirit On The Water 3 Rollin' And Tumblin' 4 When The Deal Goes Down 5 Someday Baby 6 Workingman's Blues #2 7 Beyond The Horizon 8 Nettie Moore 9 The Levee's Gonna Break 10 Ain't Talkin'

4

AWARDS &
CHART HISTORY

★

AUSZEICHNUNGEN & CHARTPLATZIERUNGEN

RÉCOMPENSES ET HISTORIQUE DES VENTES

UNITED STATES CERTIFICATIONS

The Freewheelin' Bob Dylan – Platinum / *The Times They Are A-Changin'* – Gold / *Another Side Of Bob Dylan* – Gold / *Bringing It All Back Home* – Platinum / *Highway 61 Revisited* – Platinum / *Blonde On Blonde* – Double Platinum / *John Wesley Harding* – Platinum / *Nashville Skyline* – Platinum / *Self Portrait* – Gold / *New Morning* – Gold / *Bob Dylan's Greatest Hits Volume II* – 5 Times Platinum / *Pat Garrett And Billy The Kid* – Gold / *Dylan* – Gold / *Planet Waves* – Gold / *Before The Flood* – Platinum / *Blood On The Tracks* – Double Platinum / *The Basement Tapes* – Gold / *Desire* – Double Platinum / *Hard Rain* – Gold / *Street Legal* – Gold / *Slow Train Coming* – Platinum / *Bob Dylan At Budokan* – Gold / *Dylan And The Dead* – Gold / *Infidels* – Gold / *Biograph* – Platinum / *The Bootleg Series, Volumes 1–3: Rare And Unreleased* – Gold / *MTV Unplugged* – Gold / *Bob Dylan's Greatest Hits, Volume 3* – Gold / *Time Out Of Mind* – Platinum / *The Bootleg Series, Volume 4: Live 1966—The Royal Albert Hall Concert* – Gold / *The Essential Bob Dylan* – Platinum / *Love And Theft* – Gold / *The Bootleg Series, Volume 5: Live 1975—The Rolling Thunder Revue* – Gold / *The Bootleg Series, Volume 7: No Direction Home—The Soundtrack* – Gold

UNITED KINGDOM CERTIFICATIONS

Planet Waves – Silver / *Before The Flood* – Silver / *Blood On The Tracks* – Gold / *The Basement Tapes* – Gold / *Desire* – Gold / *Hard Rain* – Gold / *Street Legal* – Platinum / *Slow Train Coming* – Gold / *Bob Dylan At Budokan* – Gold / *Saved* – Silver / *Shot Of Love* – Silver / *Infidels* – Silver / *Oh Mercy* – Gold / *Under The Red Sky* – Silver / *Time Out Of Mind* – Gold / *The Best Of Bob Dylan* – Gold / *The Essential Bob Dylan* – Platinum

GRAMMY AWARDS

Album of the Year *(The Concert For Bangladesh)*— Contributing Artist – 1972 / Best Rock Vocal Performance, Male *(Gotta Serve Somebody)* – 1979 / Best Traditional Folk Album *(World Gone Wrong)* – 1994 / Best Rock Vocal Performance, Male *(Cold Irons Bound)* – 1996 / Best Contemporary Folk Album *(Time Out Of Mind)* – 1997 / Album of the Year *(Time Out Of Mind)* – 1997 / Best Contemporary Folk Album *(Love And Theft)* – 2001 / Best Contemporary Folk/Americana Album *(Modern Times)* – 2006 / Best Solo Rock Vocal Performance *(Someday Baby)* – 2006

GRAMMY HALL OF FAME

Blowin' In The Wind – 1994 / *Like A Rolling Stone* – 1998 / *Blonde On Blonde* – 1999 / *Mr. Tambourine Man* – 2002 / *Highway 61 Revisited* – 2002 / *Bringing It All Back Home* – 2006

MISCELLANEOUS AWARDS

Tom Paine Award, National Emergency Civil Liberties Committee – 1963 / Honorary Doctorate of Music Degree, Princeton University – 1970 / **Rolling Stone** Music Award, Artist of the Year (tied with Bruce Springsteen) – 1975 / **Rolling Stone** Music Award, Album of the Year *(The Basement Tapes* and *Blood On The Tracks)* – 1975 / Mannheim-Heidelberg International Filmfestival InterFilm Award ("Renaldo And Clara") – 1978 / Dove Award, Album by a Secular Artist *(Slow Train Coming)* – 1980 / Inducted into Songwriters Hall of Fame – 1982 / Inducted into the Rock and Roll Hall of Fame – 1988 / Commandeur dans l'Ordre des Arts et des Lettres from the French Minister of Culture – 1990 / Lifetime Achievement Award, National Academy of Recording Arts and Sciences – 1991 / Arts Award, Dorothy and Lillian Gish Prize Trust – 1997 / Lifetime Achievement Award, John F. Kennedy Center Honors – 1997 / Polar Music Prize – 2000 / Golden Globe Award, Best Original Song *(Things Have Changed)* – 2000 / Academy Award, Best Original Song *(Things Have Changed)* – 2001 / Sierra Award, Las Vegas Film Critics Society Awards, Best Song *(Things Have Changed)* – 2000 / Nashville Songwriters Hall of Fame – 2002 / Honorary Doctorate of Music Degree, St. Andrews' University – 2004 / Prince of Asturias Award – 2006 / Pulitzer Prize, Special Citation – 2008

US CHART HISTORY

US CHART SINGLES

Week of Entry	Highest Position	Wks	Title	Catalog Number
36 (March 27, 1965)	9 (April 17, 1965)	11	Times They Are A-Changin'	CBS 201751
35 (May 1, 1965)	9 (May 22, 1965)	9	Subterranean Homesick Blues	CBS 201753
40 (June 19, 1965)	22 (July 3, 1965)	8	Maggie's Farm	CBS 201781
42 (August 21, 1965)	4 (September 18, 1965)	12	Like A Rolling Stone	CBS 201811
39 (October 30, 1965)	8 (December 4, 1965)	12	Positively 4th Street	CBS 201824
17 (January 29, 1966)	17 (January 29, 1966)	5	Can You Please Crawl Out Your Window	CBS 201900
44 (April 16, 1966)	33 (May 7, 1966)	5	One Of Must Know	CBS 202053
32 (May 14, 1966)	7 (June 4, 1966)	8	Rainy Day Women #12 & 35	CBS 202307
32 (July 23, 1966)	16 (August 13, 1966)	9	I Want You	CBS 202258
50 (May 17, 1969)	30 (June 7, 1969)	6	I Threw It All Away	CBS 4219
30 (September 13, 1969)	5 (October 11, 1969)	12	Lay Lady Lay	CBS 4434
47 (July 10, 1971)	24 (August 7, 1971)	9	Watching The River Flow	CBS 7329
34 (October 6, 1973)	14 (November 3, 1973)	9	Knockin' On Heaven's Door	CBS 1762
43 (February 7, 1976)	43 (February 7, 1976)	4	Hurricane	CBS 3878
40 (July 29, 1978)	13 (August 19, 1978)	11	Baby Stop Crying	CBS S CBS 6499
67 (October 28, 1978)	56 (November 4, 1978)	3	Is Your Love In Vain	CBS 6718
33 (May 20, 1995)	33 (May 20, 1995)	2	Dignity	Columbia 6620762
64 (July 11, 1998)	64 (July 11, 1998)	1	Love Sick	Columbia 6659972
58 (October 14, 2000)	58 (October 14, 2000)	1	Things Have Changed	Columbia 6693792

US CHART ALBUMS

Week of Entry	Highest Position	Wks	Title	Catalog Number
125 (September 7, 1963)	22 (October 5, 1963)	32	The Freewheelin' Bob Dylan	Columbia 8786
109 (March 7, 1964)	20 (April 18, 1964)	21	The Times They Are A-Changin'	Columbia 8905
148 (September 19, 1964)	43 (December 5, 1964)	41	Another Side Of Bob Dylan	Columbia 8993
116 (May 1, 1965)	6 (October 9, 1965)	43	Bringing It All Back Home	Columbia 9128
89 (October 2, 1965)	3 (November 6, 1965)	47	Highway 61 Revisited	Columbia 9189
101 (July 23, 1966)	9 (October 1, 1966)	34	Blonde On Blonde	Columbia 841
136 (May 6, 1967)	10 (June 17, 1967)	99	Greatest Hits	Columbia 9463
196 (January 27, 1968)	2 (February 17, 1968)	52	John Wesley Harding	Columbia 9463
22 (May 3, 1969)	3 (May 24, 1969)	47	Nashville Skyline	Columbia 9604
200 (July 4, 1970)	4 (July 25, 1970)	22	Self-Portrait	Columbia 30050
26 (November 14, 1970)	7 (December 5, 1970)	23	New Morning	Columbia 30290
30 (December 11, 1971)	14 (January 22, 1972)	31	Bob Dylan's Greatest Hits, Vol. 2	Columbia 31120
171 (August 4, 1973)	16 (October 27, 1973)	30	Pat Garrett And Billy The Kid	Columbia 32460
106 (December 22, 1973)	17 (February 2, 1974)	15	Dylan	Columbia 32747
19 (February 9, 1974)	1 (February 16, 1974)	21	Planet Waves	Asylum 1003
42 (July 13, 1974)	3 (August 3, 1974)	19	Before The Flood*	Asylum 201
15 (February 8, 1975)	1 (March 1, 1975)	24	Blood On The Tracks	Columbia 33235
58 (July 26, 1975)	7 (September 6, 1975)	14	The Basement Tapes*	Columbia PC 33682
23 (January 24, 1976)	1 (February 7, 1976)	35	Desire	Columbia PC 33893
72 (October 2, 1976)	17 (October 30, 1976)	12	Hard Rain	Columbia PC 34349
58 (July 8, 1978)	11 (August 12, 1978)	23	Street-Legal	Columbia JC 35453
96 (May 12, 1979)	13 (June 16, 1979)	25	Bob Dylan At Budokan	Columbia 36067
57 (September 8, 1979)	3 (September 22, 1979)	26	Slow Train Coming	Columbia 36120
58 (July 12, 1980)	24 (August 2, 1980)	11	Saved	Columbia 36553
59 (September 5, 1981)	33 (September 26, 1981)	9	Shot Of Love	Columbia 37496
71 (November 19, 1983)	20 (December 3, 1983)	24	Infidels	Columbia 38819

Week of Entry	Highest Position	Wks	Title	Catalog Number
122 (January 5, 1985)	115 (January 19, 1985)	9	Real Live	Columbia 39944
65 (June 22, 1985)	33 (July 13, 1985)	17	Empire Burlesque	Columbia 40110
103 (December 7, 1985)	33 (January 11, 1986)	22	Biograph	Columbia 38830
80 (August 2, 1986)	53 (August 23, 1986)	13	Knocked Out Loaded	Columbia 40439
134 (June 18, 1988)	61 (July 2, 1988)	10	Down In The Groove	Columbia 40957
80 (February 18, 1989)	37 (March 4, 1989)	11	Dylan And The Dead**	Columbia 45056
65 (October 7, 1989)	30 (October 28, 1989)	23	Oh Mercy	Columbia 45281
75 (September 29, 1990)	38 (October 6, 1990)	11	Under The Red Sky	Columbia CK 46794
76 (April 13, 1991)	49 (April 20, 1991)	6	The Bootleg Series Volumes 1-3: Rare And Unreleased 1961-1991	Columbia 86572
51 (November 21, 1992)	51 (November 21, 1992)	8	Good As I Been To You	Columbia 53200
40 (September 11, 1993)	40 (September 11, 1993)	11	The 30th Anniversary Concert Collection	Columbia 53230
70 (November 13, 1993)	70 (November 13, 1993)	4	World Gone Wrong	Columbia 57590
126 (December 3, 1994)	126 (December 3, 1994)	2	Greatest Hits Volume 3	Columbia 66783
23 (May 20, 1995)	23 (May 20, 1995)	10	MTV Unplugged	Columbia 67000
10 (October 18, 1997)	10 (October 18, 1997)	29	Time Out Of Mind	Columbia CK 68556
31 (October 31, 1998)	31 (October 31, 1998)	5	Bob Dylan Live 1966 The "Royal Albert Hall" Concert	Columbia/Legacy C2K 65759
67 (November 18, 2000)	67 (November 18, 2000)	22	The Essential Bob Dylan	Columbia C2K 85168
5 (September 29, 2001)	5 (September 29, 2001)	26	Love And Theft	Columbia CK 86076
56 (December 14, 2002)	56 (December 14, 2002)	9	The Bootleg Series Volume 5: Bob Dylan Live 1975 The Rolling Thunder Revue	Legacy/Columbia: 87047
28 (April 17, 2004)	28 (April 17, 2004)	4	The Bootleg Series Volume 6: Live 1964—The Philharmonic Hall Concert	Legacy/Columbia 86882
16 (September 17, 2005)	16 (September 17, 2005)	11	The Bootleg Series Volume 7: No Direction Home— The Soundtrack	Legacy/Columbia 93937
1 (September 16, 2006)	1 (September 16, 2006)	16	Modern Times	Columbia 87606
36 (October 20, 2007)	36 (October 20, 2007)	9	Dylan	Legacy/Columbia 05928
93 (October 20, 2007)	93 (October 20, 2007)	1	Dylan—Deluxe Edition	Legacy/Columbia 10954
6 (October 25, 2008)	6 (October 25, 2008)	6	The Bootleg Series Volume 8: Tell Tale Signs—Rare And Unreleased 1989-2006	Legacy/Columbia 35795

*with The Band
**with The Grateful Dead

UK CHART HISTORY

UK CHART SINGLES

Week of Entry	Highest Position	Wks	Title	Catalog Number
91 (July 24, 1965)	2 (September 4, 1965)	12	Like A Rolling Stone	Columbia 43346
66 (October 2, 1965)	7 (November 6, 1965)	9	Positively 4th Street	Columbia 43389
83 (April 3, 1965)	39 (May 15, 1965)	8	Subterranean Homesick Blues	Columbia 43242
71 (April 16, 1966)	2 (May 21, 1966)	10	Rainy Day Women #12 & 35	Columbia 43592
90 (July 2, 1966)	20 (July 30, 1966)	7	I Want You	Columbia 43683
99 (January 1, 1966)	58 (January 29, 1966)	6	Can You Please Crawl Out Your Window	Columbia 43477
81 (September 10, 1966)	33 (October 8, 1966)	6	Just Like A Woman	Columbia 43792
90 (May 20, 1967)	81 (June 3, 1967)	4	Leopard-Skin Pill-Box Hat	Columbia 44069
94 (July 12, 1969)	7 (September 6, 1969)	14	Lay Lady Lay	Columbia 44926
85 (November 1, 1969)	50 (November 29, 1969)	7	Tonight I'll Be Staying Here With You	Columbia 4-45004
99 (May 17, 1969)	85 (June 7, 1969)	5	I Threw It All Away	Columbia 4-44826
74 (July 25, 1970)	41 (August 15, 1970)	7	Wigwam	Columbia 4-45199
78 (June 26, 1971)	41 (August 7, 1971)	8	Watching The River Flow	Columbia 4-45409
93 (December 4, 1971)	33 (January 8, 1972)	8	George Jackson	Columbia 4-45516
80 (September 1, 1973)	12 (October 27, 1973)	16	Knockin' On Heaven's Door	Columbia 4-45913
90 (December 15, 1973)	55 (January 12, 1974)	7	A Fool Such As I	Columbia 4-45982
73 (February 23, 1974)	44 (March 23, 1974)	6	On A Night Like This	Asylum 11033
85 (August 10, 1974)	66 (August 31, 1974)	5	Most Likely You Go Your Way (And I'll Go Mine)	Asylum 11043
74 (March 8, 1975)	31 (April 5, 1975)	7	Tangled Up In Blue	Columbia 3-10106
86 (November 29, 1975)	33 (January 10, 1976)	11	Hurricane	Columbia 3-10245
74 (March 13, 1976)	54 (April 10, 1976)	5	Mozambique	Columbia 3-10298
90 (September 8, 1979)	24 (November 3, 1979)	12	Gotta Serve Somebody	Columbia 1-11072
90 (December 17, 1983)	55 (January 28, 1984)	9	Sweetheart Like You	Columbia 38-04301

UK CHART ALBUMS

Week of Entry	Highest Position	Wks	Title	Catalog Number
14 (November 21, 1964)	8 (May 8, 1965)	19	Another Side Of Bob Dylan	CBS S 62429
13 (July 18, 1964)	13 (July 18, 1964)	8	Bob Dylan	CBS S 62022
20 (July 11, 1964)	4 (May 1, 1965)	20	The Times They Are A-Changin'	CBS S 62251
17 (May 23, 1964)	1 (April 17, 1965)	48	The Freewheelin' Bob Dylan	CBS S 62193
19 (May 15, 1965)	1 (May 29, 1965)	29	Bringing It All Back Home	CBS SBPG 62515
18 (October 9, 1965)	4 (November 27, 1965)	15	Highway 61 Revisited	CBS S 62572
11 (August 20, 1966)	3 (September 3, 1966)	15	Blonde On Blonde	CBS DDP 66012
39 (January 14, 1967)	6 (March 18, 1967)	82	Greatest Hits	CBS SBPG 62847
25 (March 2, 1968)	1 (March 9, 1968)	29	John Wesley Harding	CBS SBPG 63252
6 (May 17, 1969)	1 (May 24, 1969)	42	Nashville Skyline	CBS 63601
1 (July 11, 1970)	1 (July 11, 1970)	15	Self Portrait	CBS 66250
1 (November 28, 1970)	1 (November 28, 1970)	14	New Morning	CBS 69001
40 (December 25, 1971)	12 (January 8, 1972)	15	More Bob Dylan Greatest Hits	CBS 67238/9
30 (September 29, 1973)	29 (November 24, 1973)	11	Pat Garrett And Billy The Kid	CBS 69042
35 (July 13, 1974)	8 (July 20, 1974)	7	Before The Flood*	Asylum IDBD 1
11 (February 23, 1974)	7 (March 9, 1974)	8	Planet Waves	Island ILPS 9261
9 (February 15, 1975)	4 (March 1, 1975)	16	Blood On The Tracks	CBS 69097
12 (July 26, 1975)	8 (August 2, 1975)	10	The Basement Tapes*	CBS 88147
4 (January 31, 1976)	3 (February 7, 1976)	36	Desire	CBS 86003
16 (October 9, 1976)	3 (October 16, 1976)	7	Hard Rain	CBS 86016

Week of Entry	Highest Position	Wks	Title	Catalog Number
22 (July 1, 1978)	2 (July 8, 1978)	20	**Street-Legal**	CBS 86067
6 (May 26, 1979)	4 (June 2, 1979)	19	**Bob Dylan At Budokan**	CBS 96004
2 (September 8, 1979)	2 (September 8, 1979)	13	**Slow Train Coming**	CBS 86095
5 (June 28, 1980)	3 (July 5, 1980)	8	**Saved**	CBS 86113
6 (August 29, 1981)	6 (August 29, 1981)	8	**Shot Of Love**	CBS 85178
9 (November 12, 1983)	9 (November 12, 1983)	12	**Infidels**	CBS 25539
54 (December 15, 1984)	54 (December 15, 1984)	2	**Real Live**	CBS 26334
11 (June 22, 1985)	11 (June 22, 1985)	6	**Empire Burlesque**	CBS 86313
35 (August 2, 1986)	35 (August 2, 1986)	5	**Knocked Out Loaded**	CBS 86326
32 (June 25, 1988)	32 (June 25, 1988)	3	**Down In The Groove**	CBS 4602671
99 (April 23, 1988)	47 (September 23, 1995)	3	**Greatest Hits Volume 3**	CBS 4609071
38 (February 18, 1989)	38 (February 18, 1989)	3	**Dylan And The Dead****	CBS 463381
6 (October 14, 1989)	6 (October 14, 1989)	7	**Oh Mercy**	CBS 4658001
13 (September 29, 1990)	13 (September 29, 1990)	3	**Under The Sky**	CBS 4671881
32 (April 13, 1991)	32 (April 13, 1991)	5	**The Bootleg Series Volumes 1-3**	Columbia 4680861
18 (November 14, 1992)	18 (November 14, 1992)	3	**Good As I Been To You**	Columbia 4727102
35 (November 20, 1993)	35 (November 20, 1993)	2	**World Gone Wrong**	Columbia 4748572
10 (April 29, 1995)	10 (April 29, 1995)	5	**MTV Unplugged**	Columbia 4783742
8 (June 14, 1997)	6 (June 21, 1997)	18	**The Best Of Bob Dylan**	Columbia SONYTV 28CD
10 (October 11, 1997)	10 (October 11, 1997)	6	**Time Out Of Mind**	Columbia 4869362
19 (October 24, 1998)	19 (October 24, 1998)	2	**Bob Dylan Live 1966 - The "Royal Albert Hall" Concert**	Legacy 4914852
22 (May 20, 2000)	22 (May 20, 2000)	2	**Best Of—Volume 2**	Columbia 4983612
3 (September 22, 2001)	3 (September 22, 2001)	5	**Love And Theft**	Columbia 5043642
9 (June 2, 2001)	9 (June 2, 2001)	19	**The Essential Bob Dylan**	Columbia STVCD 116
69 (December 7, 2002)	69 (December 7, 2002)	1	**The Bootleg Series Volume 5: Bob Dylan Live 1975 The Rolling Thunder Revue**	Columbia 5101403
33 (April 10, 2004)	33 (April 10, 2004)	1	**The Bootleg Series Volume 6: Live 1964—The Philharmonic Hall Concert**	Columbia 5123582
21 (September 17, 2005)	21 (September 17, 2005)	5	**No Direction Home— The Soundtrack**	Columbia 5203582
3 (September 9, 2006)	3 (September 9, 2006)	12	**Modern Times**	Columbia 82876876062
10 (October 13, 2007)	10 (October 13, 2007)	6	**Dylan**	Columbia 88697109542
9 (October 18, 2008)	9 (October 18, 2008)	3	**The Bootleg Series Volume 8: Tell Tale Signs—Rare And Unreleased 1989-2006**	Columbia 88697347472

*with The Band
**with The Grateful Dead

BIBLIOGRAPHY

Cott, Jonathan: *Bob Dylan, The Essential Interviews.*
Wenner Books, 2006.
Crampton, Luke & Dafydd Rees: *Rock & Roll.*
Year By Year. Dorling Kindersley, 2003.
Dylan, Bob: *Chronicles.* Simon & Schuster. 2004.
Heylin, Clinton: *Bob Dylan. Behind The Shades*
Revisited. William Morrow, 2001.

Santelli, Robert: *The Bob Dylan Scrapbook -*
1956-1966. Simon & Schuster, 2005.
Scaduto, Anthony: *Bob Dylan.* Grosset & Dunlap, 1972.
Shelton, Robert: *No Direction Home. The Life And*
Music Of Bob Dylan. Da Capo Press, 2003.
Sloman, Larry: *On The Road With Bob Dylan.*
Three Rivers Press, 2002.

IMPRINT

© 2009 TASCHEN GmbH
Hohenzollernring 53, D-50672 Köln
www.taschen.com

Editor: Luke Crampton & Dafydd Rees/
Original Media/www.orginal-media.net
Picture Research: Dafydd Rees & Wellesley Marsh
Editorial Coordination:
Florian Kobler and Mischa Gayring, Cologne
Production Coordination:
Nadia Najm and Horst Neuzner, Cologne
Design: Sense/Net, Andy Disl and Birgit Eichwede, Cologne
German Translation: Anke Burger, Berlin
French Translation: Alice Pétillot, Paris
Multilingual Production: www.arnaudbriand.com, Paris

Printed in Italy
ISBN 978-3-8365-1126-1

To stay informed about upcoming TASCHEN titles, please
request our magazine at www.taschen.com/magazine or write
to TASCHEN, Hohenzollernring 53, D-50672 Cologne,
Germany; contact@taschen.com; Fax: +49-221-254919. We will
be happy to send you a free copy of our magazine, which is
filled with information about all of our books.

ACKNOWLEDGMENTS

Anne-Taylor Adams, Katherine Barna, Mitch Blank, John
Byrne Cooke, Jasen Emmons at the Experience Music
Project, Ralf Gärtner, Dave Hall, Meri Hartford, Bob Korn,
Jörg Krings, Beth Lamont, Joe Medina, Barry Ollman,
Michelle Press, Silke Maria Schmidt, Joelle Sedlmeyer,
Rowland Scherman, Jochen Sperber, Sam Teicher, Claudia
Weissberg, Jon Wilton.

COPYRIGHT